The House at the Edge of the World

Tim Haynes

A land of fog and gloom…beyond it is the Sea of Death, where Hell begins."

Homer, The Iliad

ISBN: 978-1-7358138-5-1

Cover design: Derek Hewitt
Published in the United States of America
ALH Projects Inc.
9845 SW 124 Terrace Miami FL 33176

DEDICATION

For Clare, Ciaran and Gina

We can laugh about it now…can't we?

Irish/English Glossary

guards	the Garda - the police
white squad	the customs police
ditch	an obstacle, usually a wall or hedge. Not a hole.
eedjit	idiot
a land	a smack, a punch
an Almighty land	a good hiding
cute	clever at someone else's expense in a slightly devious kind of way
sally	willow tree
desperate	terrible, horrible
feck	substitute 'u' for 'e'.
hoor	whore
cratur	creature
spud/shpud	potato, exploded potato, mashed potato
sound	solid, reliable
grand	excellent
clifted	to fall to one's death off a cliff
divil	devil
shite	trouble, shit
ye	you or you plural
at all, at all	no doubt about it at all
craic	fun
handy	small but usefull
boreen	track or path
wake	lamentation and merrymaking by corpse before burial
stations	house blessing
turf	peat, partly carbonised vegetable matter used for fuel
set	an Irish square dance
slean	hand tool for cutting turf
blagard	blackguard: scoundrel
poitin	powerful illicit brew
stoops/shtoops	piles of blocks of turf
nerves	any type or number of mental illness or affliction
puk	wild goat

ACKNOWLEDGMENTS

With great appreciation to the people who made this story.

They know who they are.

And thanks to Maggie for making this book happen.

1. THE DECISION: KNOCKING ON HEAVEN'S DOOR

EVEN as we drew up outside O'Grady's pub in Glencar and witnessed, for the first time, what passed for responsible driving in the backbogs of Ireland, I knew I wanted to live here.

As I cut the engine, two men stumbled out of the pub and lurched through the beating rain towards a battered Ford Escort. In truth, one of them was beyond stumbling: his knees had buckled from the weight of liquid in his belly, the spirit of which had risen to attack that part of the brain which kept his legs supporting his body. His weaving friend carried him to the car, propped him against it with knee and elbow, and wrenched the driver's door open with his free hand. The man then dropped the dead drunk into the seat like a sack of spuds and bent down to lift his mate's useless legs, one by one, into the cab. Finally, this Good Samaritan rummaged through the Escort owner's pockets, found the right key and helpfully slipped it into the ignition. Slamming the driver's door shut, he staggered back through the rain and disappeared inside the pub. The windows of the car were all fogged up, and for a minute, there was no sound from the car or its occupant. We were just beginning to hope that the man had passed out, when the engine roared to life, and the Escort

1

bucked forward into the road, zigzagging away towards the misty mountains of Macgillycuddy Reeks. Though we didn't yet know it, the local response – if any – would have been sanguine. "Ah, what harm – only mountains and sheep out there."

We had been tooling around south west Ireland on our annual holidays for three days, enough time for the process of recuperation to be giving way to the process of taking stock. Taking stock of our last ten years in London, of a lifestyle that had become boring in its predictability. Clare and I had been doing our sums on the trip of life, and once the dissatisfactions had been aired for the thousandth time, we meandered from taking stock to having a little dream.

'I could live here,' I announced unexpectedly.

Clare was caught off guard by my tone, which sounded ominously like planning rather than dreaming.

'Here! Where? On that rock?' she said sarcastically, waving her arms in the air.

I was indeed sitting on a rock; a rock on a high cliff, with white-topped waves crashing far below and black heaving seas further out. The islands of the Ballinskelligs could just be seen with their dark, sharp towers of rock piercing the ocean's haze. Once, monks had lived there in spiritual isolation in dark and airy stone beehive dwellings. They collected water that fell from the heavens, and grew little in the flinty, unyielding soil.

The rock was on the lands west of Cahirciveen, at the end of the Iveragh Peninsula, in the County of Kerry, Republic of Ireland, overlooking the Atlantic, next stop USA. It was on the edge. London was in the middle, but for me being in the middle had become too hectic. I wanted to be on the edge – not the "edge" in the fashionable sense where new and cool things crackle and pop, but on the edge where one might experience some of the heaven in which David Byrne once suggested nothing ever happens.

Really, I was mentally searching for any place that seemed to offer a little peace and quiet; a place where everyday doesn't begin with the radio alarm telling you how terrible the world is, followed by a semi-conscious rush to work and a fight all the way through the day, your reward an exhausted flop in front of the TV before it starts over again.

Why do we do it? Why not find a place where everyday isn't a crisis, where things go round and round on their own. A place where you know what's been, and you know what's coming. Then you can relax and do something creative.

Well, that's how I put it to Clare. The discussion wasn't exactly new. Clare and I had engaged before in idle chat about the attractions of very early retirement – we were both under thirty at the time. But now, sitting out there on that rock, on holiday, in a state of mind spacious enough to contemplate ingenuity beyond catching the tube before rush hour, the idea of making a complete break with the city did not seem so far-fetched.

Drizzle was blowing in from the sea. The air tasted clean and lightly salted. We wrenched ourselves away from the solitude of that rock and walked the half mile back to the car.

We were hungry and needed to start looking for a place to stay for the night. Spreading the map between us, we chose a road which cut through the middle of the peninsula and showed several miniature blue lakes and green trees denoting the forests through which it passed. We drove through Waterville being lashed by a storm straight off the Atlantic. We ascended a hairpin pass to the top of the Ballaghisheen, sandwiched between the peaks of Knocknagapple and Knocknacusha. From which vantage we appeared to be on the lip of a huge crater edged in mist. A thin ribbon of road, more like a track, wound down into the crater, eventually being lost from view. I felt cleansed, filtered by that ever-present fine spray that stuck to the hair in beads so small they never even broke.

We plunged down the pass and into the crater, through the boglands, and then passing occasional farms with barns and stone cottages and deep mud churned up by the permanent wet and animals' hooves. We stopped at the pub in Glencar - where we witnessed the episode with the drunks in the car park - before repairing to the bar.

The Guinness was a new revelation in the consumption of alcohol, the cheese sandwich awful and the landlord unhelpful vis-à-vis the search for a place for the night. So we rolled out of 'town' half an hour later. Taking advice from the Ordinance Survey map, the scale of which was large enough to show even the houses as tiny blocks, we followed the line of a road which appeared to end abruptly against three sharply rising mountains. Half-an-hour of twisting down a track the width of our small car, brought us to what seemed like the end of the world: The land of Bridia

We were on the side of a steep mountain dropping down into a valley at the bottom of which was a river and a sharp slope up the other side. Ahead we were blocked against a steep mountain as well, over which was marked 'Black Valley'. The mist came down to a point just above our heads, so tangible we could touch it. There was a gentle hiss of distant water and the mountain was high enough to make one whisper so as not to disturb the peace with an echo.

I returned to the car and pulled out the map, which I remembered showed some houses above the road. Sure enough not fifty meters from where we stood, hidden by huge gray rocks and overgrown with all manner of fuchsia and briar, was an old cottage.

We made our way up to it on foot, slipping and sliding up what used to be a serviceable track. The cottage was derelict, and had been for some time. We pushed open a rickety door on broken hinges - and my mind went wild imagining how it once was, and how it could still be. Leave it the way it is, but make it a home.

'Now this is what I'm talking about,' I said to Clare, 'we could get some peace and quiet here."

'It's a beautiful spot, I can't argue with that," she reluctantly agreed, 'but half an hour's drive to reach another human being? That's a rather radical idea of retirement, isn't it? I mean, let's just drop out like ordinary people. Why must you always do things by extremes?'

Having always considered myself to be a man not of extremes so much as of no half measures, I ignored this rhetorical question. Anyhow, we still needed a place to stay for the night.

Scampering back to the car, we passed a turn to Dromteewakeen, and through the junction to Ballagbeama Gap between the twin-peaks of Knockaunattin and Mullaghnattin. Then we drove through the forest and up the pass alongside the stream flowing out of Lough Acoose. We crossed the plateau before the long descent down to Killorglin. Looming out of the mist and rain before the descent, a painted rock told us 'bungalow to rent'. The timing was perfect. We took the arrowed track and soon came to the bungalow, grandly named Lakeview House.

It was clear from the startled look on the face of the woman in thick jumper, dirty pants and dung soiled wellies who emerged from a backyard shed that she hadn't had tenants for some time, nor did she expect any. But Biddy Boon was pleased to give us possession of her house for a few days, and immediately we struck up a happy rapport with her. She set a turf fire in the grate while we unpacked the luggage and then all settled down to a cup of tea.

'I can't help noticing old cottages all over the country, are they abandoned or do they get used?' I thought it worth making inquiries.

'Farmers use them for gathering the sheep until they eventually fall down,' Biddy said.

I pressed on: 'Do you think a farmer would sell one?'

Biddy was nonplussed: 'Now who in God's name and their right mind would buy such a thing?'

'Well,' I drawled casually, wanting neither to offend her by blasphemy or insanity so early in our acquaintance, 'it could be a nice place to spend a holiday.' And that was the end of the topic for one night.

The following day Clare and I took a walk up the mountain behind Lakeview House and later down to Lough Acoose. The tranquillity was beginning to seep in. We returned to the bungalow and once again put our feet up in front of the turf fire.

Biddy Boon, our temporary landlady, dropped in for a chat. The conversation was becoming more personal until finally Biddy asked 'so are the two of yous married then?' At precisely the same instant I said yes and Clare said no. In a fit of general embarrassment we all started talking at once, Clare and I trying to explain the confusion over our status, Biddy saying that although it was a Catholic country, she didn't really mind these modern ways of doing things.

Before the evening was through I had resumed our chat about old stone cottages.

This time Biddy took a practical approach to the subject: 'Why don't you go and see Jack Mullane about his cottage down in Dromleagh? It's on a piece of land which was owned by Jack's brother who died 25 years ago, and they don't really take much interest in the place anymore. I can call him and you could see the place tomorrow. There couldn't be any harm in that now.'

Jack and Peig Mullane were an utterly lovable couple. She was eighty, he was seventy five, and the obvious love and respect he showed her isn't often seen – certainly not in the depths of rural Ireland. Their cottage was five miles from the sea by picturesque road through mountains and woodlands. But Jack had never been to the sea. He was tall, thin faced with full silver gray hair topped with a hat that sat on his head for the last thirty years at least. The plastic plate which was his teeth had also been in there a good few decades by the looks of the gap – into which his pipe fitted perfectly – that had been worn away. Before starting on the dentures, the pipe had worn away the teeth in exactly the same fashion. When the pipe got too hot, Jack let it rest while he had an Old Holborn rollup. He described how he'd smoked his first fag at eight, was hooked at ten, and took to the pipe at fifteen. It was customary in those parts for smokers to flick cigarette ash into the tops of their wellington boots when indoors, and I could only wonder how many pairs of Jack's wellies had been filled up this way.

Jack Mullane literally had a twinkle in his bright, sharp eyes. He would listen carefully and make acute comments - not based on a storehouse of worldly knowledge, but on long years of observation and experience of the human race. Coupled with a great wit, he was stimulating fireside company, and he liked nothing better than drying out in front of the little log blaze in their comfortable cottage.

Peig was small and quiet, yet there was a determined set to her. She treated everything with kindness, consequently there lounged about the place several long-haired cats with names like Flooffy and Gingy (domestic cats were a rarity in rural Ireland). They even had a sheep that from birth had been brought into the house as a pet for their grandchildren. The sheep thought it was a dog and behaved exactly like one, except that because it couldn't bark, it didn't bleat either, fearful that it would give itself away. Peig went about her business in her slippers, and when anybody or any activity began to get too exuberant, she would have her quiet but firm say and bring everything back down to earth.

Both she and Jack were very proud of their postage stamp of a garden in front of the cottage, which was filled to the brim with beautiful flowers. Every detail of Jack and Peig and their animals, cottage and garden could have been drawn from a children's storybook. Certainly, the Mullane's picture-perfect life shifted Clare's attitude to my project from being ambivalent with a touch of anti, to ambivalent with a touch of pro. This small but important change gave me the green light to steam ahead with my own retirement plan.

In one small respect was Peig ashamed of their lifestyle. Clare and I slept a night in the third room of their cottage. Before retiring Peig rolled in a little cushioned chair with grubby floral flounces tacked round the bottom like a skirt.

'If you need to, just use that,' she said with obvious embarrassment.

'Use it for what?' I asked innocently.

'Just use it,' Clare snapped.

Peig left and Clare pulled off the cushion to reveal a potty, cunningly hidden beneath the skirt's flounces. There was no toilet in the cottage.

The afternoon's business was to discuss a possible purchase price for the stone cottage at Dromleagh. There seemed to be certain rules for conducting these discussions. The first was that Jack had to act as if he didn't know what I had come to talk about, and I had to act as if he didn't know what I'd come to talk about.

Whatever the rules, it was a big day, and the excitement was palpable. The table had been properly prepared with two glasses and a little flagon of water covered by another glass. All that was lacking was a chessboard. The room had been set up so that the women were well away from the table so as not to be a distraction to the men conducting their business.

Jack was brighter than ever.

'Now come in Tim, here boy, give me that coat. Set yourself down, take the weight off those feet, tired from all this holidaying.' We all laughed.

'I get much more tired on holiday than when I'm at work,' I said continuing the theme.

'I wouldn't be knowing about that, I've never been on holidays in my life. But some would say I've never done any work either.' We all laughed again.

'Well, whatever your recipe is, you should let me have it. I would be happy to be as fit and healthy as you are when I'm ready to retire.' I said.

'A good shpud, a warm fire, a walk in the mountains, my lovely wife - you don't need much,'

'I'd be happy to retire with your lovely wife,' I said, wondering if I'd pushed risqué too far.

'I'd be happy to go,' Peig said softly with a smile.

'Take her away, she's old and good for nought' Jack laughed, ' but then you leave Clare behind.'

The first volley of pleasantries completed, Jack started twisting round in his chair.

'Now where's that bottle girl? Can't you see the man's fairly thirsting to death while we're all laughing and joking.' Peig shuffled round in her slippers and pulled out a new bottle of John Power whisky from the cabinet beneath a pile of brown, finger-worn family photographs.

Jack opened the bottle and filled my table glass to the brim. He did the same with his own.

'Some water?' he offered.

'No thanks,' I said, peering at my almost overflowing glass. What else was there to say?

He took a deep slug,

'And may you return to Kerry again and again,' he said with that twinkle.

'Thanks' I said taking a slug myself.

'Now what might it be that you would want to talk about?' he asked diplomatically.

I got straight to the point: 'How much would you want for the sale of the cottage at Dromleagh?' Jack laughed softly: 'But I never said I would be wanting even to sell the cottage at Dromleagh, not even a rock at Dromleagh or anywhere else.' He took another slug, and so did I.

So we first had to discuss if he would sell a rock before we got onto a house. The conversation became very abstract. What sort of rock? Why would he sell? Why should he sell? If he should sell, would he? If he would sell, should he? Have another slug. Why not, what the hell, we were settled in for the night.

Why sell? Maybe it's time to buy. If someone wants to buy, maybe it's time to buy, not sell. The first glass was empty, the second was filled to the brim. I wanted to get a drop of water in but was too slow seeing him lift the bottle. Jack was having fun. He threw some more logs on the fire. I loosened my collar and felt the sweat around my neck.

'Now what would someone want with a pile of rocks that's only been the resting place for sheep in twenty five years?' Thus began an analysis of what we wanted the cottage for. And this seemed like a damned strange notion to Jack, so it had to be investigated in case he was missing something that might turn out to be a platinum find under the living room floor.

I was already slurring my words, and having to justify my early retirement scheme under such conditions almost had me changing my mind. It's funny how the most ridiculous notions end up being defended the most vigorously. This took us to the end of the second straight glass of neat whisky. There was one glass each left in the bottle. He poured them out without protest from me - I was beginning to feel like a broken captive in the hands of some vicious security police.

'Now what sort of figure were you intending paying for Dromleagh?' Jack asked at last.

'Five thousand pounds is all we've got,' I managed to get out without too much of a slur.

'There's not a lot one can buy for that sort of money these days, but I tink we can do something for, say…ten.'

The horse trading began in earnest. I gave my reasons for five, he gave his reasons for ten, I countered, he parried.

The I heard his steady voice, low and serious: 'Close the gap, Tim, close the gap'

My drunken mind fixed on the Liverpool Street tube station in London. 'Mind the gap, mind the gap'. I used to look down between the platform and the train and try to imagine what it would be like down there when the train moved off.

Jack put his elbows on the table, his eyes bored into mine, and I think he repeated: 'Close the gap, Tim, close the gap'. The third glass was almost empty, the bottle was finished, if I could just last this out.

Then Jack delivered the coup de grace. Swinging round in his chair, he leaned into the cupboard and pulled out another bottle of whisky. Before he could get the top twisted off I fairly blurted across the table.

'Eight … alright … nine thousand, Jack, the gap is closed, please, let's say the deal is done and both sleep sound.'

'Tim, you're a hard man. I respect a hard man. You've forced me to let it go for nine and a half. But this has been thirsty work for someone who's on his holidays, and someone who's never done a day's work in his life. Now let's have a little drink to celebrate.' And with that the top of the second bottle came off and our glasses were filled to the brim.

The next day it was arranged for us to visit the offices of the solicitor in Killarney, who would cobble together a Letter of Intent, to convince both parties that the other was serious and would pursue the matter to finality. We set off from Lakeview House in gray mist and drizzle. Neither the mountain nor the lake were visible, nor, indeed, much of the road ahead. Driving slowly to make allowances for the mist and the odd stray cow or group of sheep that would lurch disconcertingly into view, we suddenly saw a man staggering up a grass track going off the main road. Hearing the car, he stopped and half turned, taking three or four swaying steps. His one hand was clutching the front of his pants, holding them up. The back of his pants were halfway to his knees showing a big pink butt, framed by the dark clothes and perfectly segmented in two by a black line. It was nine thirty in the morning.

Clare and I looked at each other and started to laugh.

'I've just got to come and live here,' I said, though to this day I have no idea why the sight of a drunk having a crap on the side of the road before tea time on a Tuesday morning should move me so.

Halfway down the winding pass, the Mullane's cottage at Dromleagh, the property we were on our way to buy, came into view. The traditional three-roomed cottage was directly across the valley on the same level as the road on which we were travelling. What remained of the battered red painted roof lay in stark contrast to the green of the grass and fern covered fields of the hill. Massive holly, oak and ash trees rose up behind the house, whose shabby white walls were obscured by tall nettles. The black holes of the two windows on either side of the doorway described an emptiness that beckoned to be filled. The house's very isolation seemed to imply insulation against the world's harsher realities. This spiritual evocation seemed to be given material form by the massive rock boundary walls which, though they had been breached in many places, could easily be restored to castle-like impenetrability. I wanted to rush across that valley there and then and embrace the loneliness, rip up the nettles and roll back the abandonment. Instead I contented myself by thinking that we were on our way to ensuring that the dream would not disappear by mid-morning.

'I can't believe we're doing this,' said Clare, a mixture of resignation and fear in her voice.

'Think of it like this,' I said, 'how many times does one go away on a holiday to a wonderful place and dream about staying there forever? While in that wonderful place take some simple action to ensure return at a later date. Like buying a house. Then the dream may be turned into reality, and maybe even permanent reality.'

We met Jack Mullane at the appointed place on New Street, Killarney, paradoxically one of the oldest streets in the town. He had donned his Sunday best black suit and a clean white shirt and tie. He took off his hat to shake my hand and I noticed that even his hair had been brushed in honour of the august occasion. He was with a man half his age whom he introduced as Ger, his son.

'I'm getting a bit old for these tings, so Ger looks after the farms now,' said Jack by way of introduction. Clearly, Ger too had pulled on his best clothes for the great event, for one could see how uncomfortable he was in his get-up. He stood scrunching his cap in his large, calloused hands, his smile revealing several gaps between nicotine-brown stubs. He hadn't yet qualified for the plastic plate that was his father's pride. While Jack's confidence and upright bearing gave him a respectable presence, such qualities were utterly lacking in Ger.

We entered a building which had not been refurbished, unlike many in Killarney that had benefited from the town's revival as a tourist attraction. The peeling double front doors with ancient round brass doorknob, opened onto a stairwell rising up through the middle of the building. The original grandeur of the mahogany staircase and skirtings, the pressed plaster of ceilings and cornices, were now dingily decrepit.

The offices of the attorney were on the ground floor. A thin, wizened woman opened the glass hatch, looked over her pince nez and told us Mr. O'Connor was just completing some business and would be with us shortly. Her demeanour became one of such total reverence when she mentioned the name 'O'Connor' that I felt excited at the prospect of being about to sit down in the presence of such a great personage. Snapping the glass hatch closed with quiet efficiency, Mr. O'Connor's disciple turned away in her black full length dress and white bib collar and continued to organise the pile of brown files stacked up on the ancient desk before her.

Jack and Ger stood uncomfortably, also humbled by the idea of visiting an attorney in the big town. The whole scene was positively religious, as everyone observed a church-like silence. I felt as if I had been sucked into a page of James Joyce, and was standing outside Mr. Alleyne's office in the Dubliners.

Minutes passed and a bell rang. Mr. O'Connor's secretary was up like an Exocet, gently knocking on the great man's door while motioning us to stay where we were. She disappeared inside, emerging a moment later to announce piously, 'Mr. O'Connor is ready for you now.'

The party shuffled into the tiny office. There were no windows, the lighting was fluorescent and the walls were as dark as the air was dank. An enormous desk occupied most of the space, and Mr. O'Connor - who exactly resembled Mr. Toad of Toad Hall - occupied the rest. He went through the motions of getting up to greet us, though he was quickly defeated by his enormous girth, which started at his bulbous red chin. His overlong hair was nicotine gray, and his right arm and hand permanently cradled his great gut, ensuring that his fly was sealed and his pants pulled up.

'Close the door Miss O'Rourke,' he called to his assistant.

'Certainly, Mr. O'Connor, sir.' she replied with shining obedience, as she'd probably been doing for the last forty years. I fancied that she lived in infinitely patient hope that perhaps one day, when the clients had all gone home, Mr. O'Connor would instruct her personally: 'Close the door Miss O'Rourke...I'm ready for you now.' Perhaps it was some such little fantasy that kept Mr. O'Connor's secretary slaving her life away over those musty manila files.

Mr. O'Connor searched through the files on his desk while passing pleasantries with Jack and Ger. Clearly in the long distant past he had been of service to them, and no doubt Miss O'Rourke had pulled the file in anticipation.

We discussed what needed to be done. An engineer had to be appointed to survey the land and mark the boundaries, the relevant documents had to be pulled from the land registry office, the use status of the road needed to be established as it passed through three farms, etc, etc. We all had to sign some documents, but Jack had forgotten to bring his spectacles. Mr. O'Connor kindly removed his and gave them to Jack who then signed with perfect visual clarity.

The formalities over, Mr. O'Connor rang the bell and Miss O'Rourke swung the door open so rapidly that she could only have been standing right outside.

'Show the party out Miss O'Rourke.'

'Certainly, Mr. O'Connor'.

Clare and I squinted out of the dark building into the gray light and drizzle feeling rather bizarre that in the course of a week's holiday we'd irrevocably changed the direction of our lives. Although it was to be another six years before we were able to extricate ourselves from London, we had taken the wildly spontaneous step required to prevent it from ever fading into the family album as another summer's holiday.

2. A CARAVAN OF ONE'S OWN

Rain drummed down on the van. Silver blurred visibility. I eased off the throttle until focus returned. To speed up was to get blasted by another sheet of rain. The wipers, on high speed, slapped water down one way then threw it off the other. The fan, at full tilt, whirred on the defrost setting. It was a struggle made more difficult by the van being loaded to capacity and beyond, winding narrow Irish roads and a nine month old baby between Clare and myself, strapped in and long since tired of this new adventure. We were on our way to County Kerry, to Droumleagh and the cottage we had bought some six years earlier. London was history. Our house in Finsbury Park had been rented out, only because we had been unable to sell it. Our jobs had been abandoned. Our worldly goods - save what was with us in the van - had been sold or dumped. This car journey marked our one-way passage into a new life, with no escape route provided for in the event of failure.

A superficial look at the map suggested that the drive would be a couple of hours from London to Wales and the ferry, followed by a rest and a bite to eat on the boat, then a couple of hours across Ireland. The drive both across England and Ireland are deceptive. Continual road improvement works in England and the lack of road works in Ireland conspire in the creation of a nightmare journey across both countries.

We'd timed everything to perfection. We'd exercised baby Ciaran on the ferry, wearing him out on all the kiddies' play apparatus in preparation for a sleep once we were in the van and back on the road for the last leg of the journey. It worked like a charm. Our van was near the front of the queue in the ferry's hold. As we approached the Port of Dun Laoighaire, Ciaran was strapped into his chair, and fell asleep immediately. The ferry's immense doors began to open, then shuddered to a halt. They were jammed. For the next two hours, we were a captive audience to the antics of a posse of 'travellers' in their beat up old Valiants and Vauxhalls hitched to spectacularly ornate caravans.

'Gypsies!' I hissed across the cab to Clare, much as General Custer must have announced 'Indians!' to his trusty lieutenants as he cantered into that cul-de-sac. We were later to learn that 'gypsies' and 'tinkers' were neither terms of endearment nor politically sensitive, so 'travelers' it was. We witnessed in those next two hours a life story, the emotional range of which most mortal families would have taken several years, if not decades, to emulate.

A small, spotty kid was behaving in a mildly irritating way in the narrow aisles between the cars, vans and caravans, when a bald, speckled and vertically-challenged man pulled his belt from his baggy denims and thrashed the kid so viciously that we were left in shocked silence. None of the other 'travelers' batted an eyelid. Both they and the kid had obviously been there before, for although he was limping around with red weals wherever his skin was exposed, he sought no sympathy with tears. The man disappeared for a moment, but soon returned. Now he was howling and sobbing and begging forgiveness, his face soggy with tears, wailing his undying love for the boy who, once again, was not going to try earning Brownie points from this about turn. Suddenly, the sobbing man was joined by a girl in her early twenties (the mother? the sister?), who ripped into him with flying fists and kicking feet, until he slumped down between the vans, shouting that this was exactly the sort of treatment he deserved.

And so it went on like that, back and forth, between the jammed cars and vans in the dark, sweaty hold of the hellish boat.

The doors of the ferry eventually swung open and released their boiling cargo. Simultaneously, baby Ciaran's eyes fluttered open. He too had released some boiling cargo requiring our immediate attendance at the roadside. All thoughts of kissing the soil of our new homeland – or at least of savouring the significant moment - were lost in a miasma of foul nappy and the search for our first Irish dustbin.

We'd taken a wrong turning, partly on account of the abominable weather, and had travelled the long way, through Cork City. The winding road through the mountains between Cork and Kerry was sheer hell. But we were now through the town of Killarney and into the home strait.

We had a vague notion that, being spring, the tourist influx of summer was yet to begin and it would be easy to find immediate accommodation, which we could use as a base to find some temporary accommodation while we rebuilt our cottage at Droumleagh. However, this vague notion did not consider the weather, the baby and our exhausted condition.

It was 2pm and between Ciaran's howls and the rain beating on the panel van, Clare and I had to shout.

"Should we go straight up to the cottage?"

"What? In this weather? It hasn't even got a proper roof!"

"Should we go to the Mullane's?"

"Ugh, I haven't got the energy for social niceties. Besides they haven't got space for us."

"Should we check into a hotel?"

"What hotel?"

"Haven't got a clue."

Clare was losing it: "I'm not driving round and round looking for a bloody hotel. I can't even see a house, let alone a hotel."

I was losing it: "I'm the one driving round and round, and if you think you're sick of it, how the hell do you think I feel?"

"Well do whatever you want to do," said Clare icily, "but I'm telling you this baby's had enough."

We both gave up. The van followed the road in the general direction of Killorglin, until I noticed a caravan park sign in the gloom. It took a couple of instants for my travel-singed brain to cotton on to its potential. A caravan could serve both our immediate and temporary accommodation needs. Why hadn't I thought of it before? A snug little home with all the cooking and ablution facilities, cheap and without responsibility, would mean we could start work on the cottage straight away. Presumably one didn't need to beat one's children senseless in public to qualify to live like the band of travellers we'd encountered on the ferry.

I pulled over to the side of the road, sliding off the edge of the tarmac into some mud. I looked forward and back, but there was no way I could turn around, the road was too narrow.

"Now what?' Clare asked.

"I've got just the solution." I said prematurely.

Ciaran had by now set up a constant wail. "Take it easy for one more minute" I said confidently.

At last I found a place wide enough for us to turn around. I opened the window and stuck my head out to look behind, sending a freezing blast of air through the van and a shower of icy water through my hair. Closing the window, the glass on the inside fogged up immediately, but at least we were headed in the direction of the caravan park. Minutes went by, but along with road visibility, the caravan park sign had simply disappeared. More minutes went by before I accepted that we must have overshot the mark. It was time to turn back again. By now Clare had joined Ciaran in a hollering chorus. I put my head down and prayed.

The "Caravan Park" sign came into view, pointing the way down a steep slope leading to an embankment studded with massive mobile homes. We slithered down the muddy road, into the middle of the deserted camp. I switched off the ignition, surprising both the baby and Clare into joint silence with the car.

"I'll be back in a second' I said, starting to feel rather pleased with myself for this upturn of events and the gratitude that was about to overwhelm me for saving the day. I hopped out the van, pulling my Parka over my head and, by sheer physical force, just managing to prevent the door from being ripped off its hinges by the wind.

Head bowed, I made my way across to what looked like the leading caravan and rapped on the door. There was no reply. I looked around and saw a shed with a block building and lean-to off the side. I peered through the window, saw nothing, and shouted 'hello'. I felt, more than saw, a figure coming towards me, looking just like me, in fact, its NATO Parka-ed head bowed against the wind, hands stretching the pockets.

'Hello" I said. We're looking for a place to stay'

'Who's we?' he asked sizing me up, unfriendly.

'Myself, my wife and a baby' I said.

'This is a caravan park."

'I know ' I tried not to get annoyed and spoil my chances. "Can't we stay here?"

'It's not open' he said.

'When will it be open?"

'In the summertime, for holidays."

'How much do they cost?" I asked hoping that if he could smell money he might be more interested.

'Five hundred punt a week, get out on Sunday afternoon,' he said.

For that I might as well have bought a caravan. There wasn't much point in pursuing the inquiry any longer, but I give it one more go.

'But we want to stay a few months, can't we make a different plan.'

'Ah, now ' he said ' we only do the holiday caravan.'

I turned miserably back to the van, wherein I had to explain my dashed hopes. The man in the Parka stood in the rain watching us take our leave up the slope and out of his caravan park, as if he wanted to make sure we were going.

'Let's go up to the Boons,' I said 'they'll be pleased to see us and maybe have some ideas about accommodation. If they don't, at least we'll get a hot cup of tea.' I was thinking that Lakeview house, the Boon's holiday bungalow where we'd first hatched our dream of living in rural Ireland, might save the day once again.

We turned left through Killorglin and headed up into the mountains. Half way up, we caught sight of our derelict stone cottage across the valley. It was that same view that had stolen my heart six years earlier. The awesome scale of our task hit me then, arousing a flash of panic. A bit late in the day, Clare would have said, if I'd confessed my feelings to her, which I didn't.

The higher up the pass we drove, the stronger the wind blew. By the time we reached the summit, the van was swaying like a fishing boat in an enormous sea. As the road leveled out to skirt round Lough Acoose, we turned off at a freshly painted arrow on a rock pointing to Lakeview House.

Ascending again, it was only a short distance to the 'bungalow.' Another hundred metres up a treacherous muddy track, stood the Boon's cottage, the original family house, tucked away, out of the path of the gale. By contrast, the new bungalow was built to look every storm coming off the Atlantic straight in the teeth. That was the way with all those bungalows, built in the Sixties with the first wave of European Community grant money that crashed on Irish shores. Sticking out like sore thumbs, wrecking fantastic landscapes, they were built of massive concrete blocks, allowing them to sit out the savage weather unmoved, but with wind rattling the glass and taking tiles off, and the wet rotting everything not concrete.

We stopped around the back of Lakeview House. I jumped out of the van and knocked on the door. There was no reply and no sign of activity. I returned to the van and sat back inside. We all felt relieved that this was an end point of some sort. We contemplated making the trip up the muddy track to the old house when a car turned off the main road and drew up to the bungalow. I stepped out of the van once again and waved at the driver.

'Conal,' I said, recognizing the Boon's eldest son.

'Yes' he said, sceptically.

'I'm Tim,' I said 'Do you remember me?'
'No' he said.

'We were here six years ago.'

"No" he said again.

I gave up on him and tried another tack: 'Where's your mother?"

'I don't know,' he said brusquely, clearly not wanting to give away too much information, an attitude that we were going to have to get used to in Ireland.

'We'll wait for her,' I turned away trying to get my body to read 'well fuck you too'.

I returned to the van, his car wound very slowly up the muddy track to the old house. Five minutes later, it came sliding back down the track and stopped next to our van. Conal stuck his head out and announced that if we wanted to wait inside, the door of the bungalow was open. Off he went again ... very slowly. That was the way with Conal. He always drove slowly. Even in the quiet of the country you never saw him coming. It suited him that he was not seen and that the fact of his presence took everyone by surprise.

We dashed inside. The kitchen was wrought in melamine, with boards swollen and tatty from the damp and years of sloppily cleaned fry-ups. Old glass fronted cupboards, fashionable in the forties, overflowed with chipped *objects d'art* - plastic ballerinas, an incomplete set of glasses with Irish coffee recipes painted on the side, all manner of scraps about Guinness and a clutch of Catholic ornaments including Jesus figurines and little nativity scenes with real straw. Jesus holding a lamb gazed benevolently out of a poster permanently illuminated from below by a special wall light. A big, ripped plastic lounge suite squatted alongside an iron table and chairs, watched over by another poster, this time of the Last Supper. The floor was lino with frayed edges, the lightbulbs a depressing 40-watt. But we were happy that silence had replaced the roar of the vehicle, happy that stillness had replaced vibration and we could re-assume control of our senses. Clare spread out the baby gear and proceeded to service all Ciaran's neglected orifices while I went in search of kettle and cups. Obviously no-one had stayed there in a good while.

It wasn't long before we heard another car coming up the slope to the house. I opened the front door just as it came to a halt. I could see Biddy and big Joe Boon through the window of the car looking at me quizzically. She got out of the car and came towards me, still looking at me with the blankly curious stare of the stranger, and my heart dropped. Jaysus, for the woman who was instrumental in persuading us to move here not to know who we are, and after the reception we got from the weather, the caravan park man and Conal to our immigration to Ireland, we might as well have driven straight back to London.

"Hello," I called.

"Now, who might ye be?" Biddy asked

"It's Tim," I said.

"Teem" she repeated, thinking.

Suddenly the penny dropped. "Teem!" she screamed with joy and ran round the car to hug me. It was a huge relief.

'Joe, for the love of Jesus, get out of the car man,' she just had time to say before disappearing inside the house to see Clare.

Big Joe pushed open the door and started pulling himself gingerly out of the car. He was an immense man. His size making the injury to his back that much more difficult to deal with. Several years earlier he had had an accident on a horse. He had been breaking in a big filly down on the field in front of Lakeview House, and the filly had bolted, surprising big Joe who had flown off the saddle but only partly hit the ground on account of one foot remaining caught up in a stirrup. The horse charged round the field, dragging big Joe behind it on his back with one leg in the air attached to the saddle. The field was flat except for a ridge of rock protruding into the middle from one side. Fortunately for big Joe, the rock was round, otherwise it would have snapped his vertebrae the first time he was scraped across it. As it was, the first crossing was sufficient to knock big Joe unconscious. And the horse just kept on galloping round and round the field. Every time it crossed the rock big Joe's body would thump across it. No-one was around to witness the accident so the horse only stopped galloping from sheer exhaustion. Though Big Joe's spine was wrecked, miraculously the cord was undamaged. Several operations later, his vertebrae were knitted together to form a solid trunk. As rigid as his torso now was, it did not stop him indulging in his favorite activities like set dancing. On several occasions we joined the valley folk on pub nights reserved for the dainty art of old Irish set dancing. Once, big Joe managed to drag Clare onto the dance floor, where he flung her around, she hanging onto his massive trunk like a leaf to an oak as an autumn wind tries to separate them.

Big Joe's daytime get-up was the standard suit pants and slightly too small jacket, white shirt and cardigan with big wellingtons on one end, and on the other, one of several styles of moth-eaten headgear, depending on the mood.

'Hallo', he said cheerfully as he enveloped my hand in his, giving it a light squeeze which had me wincing. He said something in his Kerry mountain accent which I didn't understand. This amused him. I said something in my London-tempered South African accent which he didn't understand. This didn't amuse him. We went inside.

Biddy was raving about what a big strong lad Ciaran was and then we went through the first of countless forthcoming rituals. First it was the weather, the weather yesterday and for few weeks before, then what the forecast said for the following day, low pressure still building in the Atlantic so gales to get worse but it felt a little easier than yesterday and there have been a few breaks in the cloud so maybe it will break a bit first before it gets worse. Then it was the seasons and how last summer was no real summer to speak of, a couple of days at the end of April, then just when they'd managed to skin the turf, down it came again. There was the start of what looked like it could be an Indian summer but then it faded as fast as it promised, and then there was some bitter cold although it was quite dry, thank the Almighty. January and February were deadly but not as bad as the year before, when we lost some sheep caught in snow drifts on Carrountoohil.

Then it was the turn of the sheep. Big Joe and Conal had to bring them down early off the mountain that year because there was nothing to eat, but luckily they picked up a good dog, the other two were getting old so this pup had time to learn. They only lost a couple of lambs that year to the fox, but quite a few more on account of a deadly cold snap just after they were born, whereas last year it was the other way around, many lost to the fox but fine, healthy lambs born.

Then it was onto family matters. How's Tommy? Still in London but says he's coming home soon, the little devil, and little Joe coming back for good in a month's time, he and Mary Teehan have got a daughter, Sara, now, and Vera is married to Mikey Tangney and living with his parents just down the road in Beaufort, and Breda's in London, still with that Gene Corkery, and Eoin and Nora in Kilburn, you know they had the boy with the bad ears, but Nora got a good job at the special school and Eoin's still at the cars.

"So have you been down to your house at Dromleagh?" Biddy finally asked.

"No, we've just arrived, so we were looking for a place to stay, get settled a bit first, you know with the baby and that," I said.

"You won't be getting much at this time of year," she said "but why don't you stay here while you get yourself sorted out"
"But what about you and big Joe and Conal?" I asked.

"We're all in the old house, Joe hates this bungalow and much prefers his open fire, and there's the spare room for Conal and he gets his meals up there. So he prefers the old place as well."

"We'll stay," I said greatly relieved that our journey had temporarily ended.

When our new landlords had left, Clare and I inspected the bedrooms, picked one, then removed the nylon sheets from the bed and brought duvets and Ciaran's cot from the van along with a few other necessities. Biddy came back that evening, bringing some dry turf for the fire which she promptly got going for us. She sat for an hour chatting away, and laughing in her completely over-the-top "yoo whoo whoo" way. Biddy could see fun times ahead with our presence to relieve the monotony of her lonely existence on the top of that unforgiving mountain.

Clare and I were clapped out. We fell into bed that first night, satisfied that after years of contemplation, argument, persuasion, planning and extricating ourselves from one kind of life, we'd finally arrived in another. How the rest would pan out was anybody's guess.

3. THE SHRINKING HILL

The following day we awoke to a dark, overcast sky and a cold drizzle, giving us every reason to remain snuggled up in bed. Unusually, nine month old Ciaran had slept through the night, leaving us remarkably refreshed. I made tea, brought it to bed and the three of us stayed put for the rest of the morning.

Lakeview House looked down from a slight elevation over Lough Acoose which sits just under Mount Carrountoohil, the highest peak in Ireland. Looking south-west from this height afforded a ringside seat into the teeth of the weather built over thousands of miles of the Atlantic. This was the first bit of land on which to vent gales and deposit rain before passing over the rest of Ireland, Britain and Europe. Paying little heed to pressure highs and lows, the wind and the rain were excited to be there, it swirled with a wild lack of direction that could literally knock you off your feet. One day I noticed that the rain was moving horizontally. Nothing peculiar about that, but I swear it was going left and right at the same time.

That morning the windows overlooking the gray, jumpy surface of Lough Acoose were rattling like sabres and the concrete roof tiles clacked and rumbled like sheep's hooves on stone. But nestled up in bed, it felt as if the elements conspired with us, not against us. We were in a house on a mountain, with no telephone, nobody knew where we were or how to get hold of us, and there was nothing we had to do. It was one of those rare moments in life we constantly strive for and seldom attain. Certainly it felt like a timely demonstration of the wisdom of our decision to live a more sedate life.

The peace lasted all of one day. It was not shattered by bad news or anything cataclysmic, so much as tested in the maddeningly elusive way a mosquito can ruin a good night's sleep.

Over the next few days we became aware of an intermittent drone in the distance, sometimes audible, sometimes not, depending on the direction of the wind and rain. It could be at six in the morning, noon, or eight in the evening. It was so distant and peculiar, that it took three or four days to warrant a mention. It took several more to establish the direction it was coming from. Somewhere between us and Lough Acoose, there was a machine at work - almost non-stop.

Lakeview House sat on an elevation stretching to the main road between Killorglin and Glencar. Lower down, across the road, was a derelict house. The land then rose to a hill, before undulating down to the lake. The derelict house appeared to be positioned so that the hill would take the brunt of any storm coming from the west over the lake. On top of this hill a large machine was at work, but it was altogether too far to make out any detail.

'Did we bring those binoculars?' I called to Clare.

Clare snorted: 'Six days, that's how long it's taken you to start spying on the neighbours.' She was right. In London it hadn't seemed to matter who we were living next door to, even less what they were up to. But if a pair of binoculars was the rural equivalent of twitching net curtains, I was only momentarily shamefaced about diving for them.

'Well, of course,' I said pompously. 'There's wildlife in the country that one ought to keep an eye on, and anyhow, the distances are so much greater.'

Binoculars glued to my face, I scoured the top of the hill. The topography was typically Irish. Globs of bogland on the lower ground and in the depressions, prickly yellow gorse bush higher up, covering the open land between grey rocks. The odd patch of grass, and the occasional rowan tree emerging from rocks inaccessible to sheep, completed the scene. I found and focused on an earth-moving machine on huge steel tracks, topped with a cab and a steel arm, jointed in the middle like an elbow. On the end of the arm was a large toothed bucket, carefully removing the top layer of soil and making an immense pile of it to one side of the machine. The intention appeared to be to preserve the topsoil and expose the underlying soil over the hill's considerable breadth. The top of the hill looked like the newly-shorn head of a soldier.

When there was no more topsoil a new process began. A large tractor with an enormous trailer was brought into service, and the machine began filling the trailer with scoops of gravelly earth. Whenever the trailer was full, the machine operator hopped down from the cab, started up the tractor and drove the trailer to deposit the load on the lower land behind the hill. He then returned for another load, and another.

Every now and then the bucket would scrape against a rock, sending a tooth quivering screech across the countryside. The bucket then carefully dug around the rock, establishing its size and depth. Either it would be removed when it was loose, or left standing like an unwanted carbuncle. Gradually, a Martian landscape emerged from that Irish hill as a series of huge boulders on stalks rose out of the receding earth.

The weather conditions were irrelevant to all this activity, as was the time of day. At night or early in the morning, the machines worked in the glow of the tractor's headlights. Day after day, Sundays included, man and machine remained committed to bringing down the mountain. The reason remained a mystery.

Biddy, our old friend and new landlady, was fast developing the habit of visiting at all hours of the day or night, mainly for a chat, but using any pretext - delivery of a bucket of turf for the fire, an old baby blanket for Ciaran. It wasn't long before she was once again comfy in front of the fire, and we asked her about the earth works. Though Biddy was quick to share with us the identity and provenance of the machine driver - 'Daniel Casey from Glencar' - she was reluctant to give away much detail.

'What is he doing moving that earth about on the hill, Biddy?' we asked.

Her laugh changed from the carefree *you-whoo-whoo* we were used to, to a low-pitched, guarded *yo-ho-ho*.

'Now I wouldn't be knowing that now would I?'

'But why don't you ask him, he's your neighbour after all?'

Biddy was sincerely shocked: 'So help me God, you don't ask a man his business. You might do that in whatever strange lands you come from, but here in Kerry that would be classed as nosy. Besides, Joe and him are in *dishpute*.'

'Oh' we said, not wanting to be classed as nosy before we'd even started. Fortunately though, Biddy continued.

'Daniel Casey keeps throwing our sheep off of that land, and one of them got *shtuck* in the ditch and died. And if it happens again, Joe might just go down there with the boys and give that cute fecker an almighty land.'

'Who owns that ground down there?' I asked, risking further admonishment.

Biddy cheeks flushed red. The deepening furrow between her eyebrows told us she was uncomfortable: she had allowed her emotions to set her tongue wagging and now she regretted it.

'It's difficult to say, the owner of that land went to America some years back so we don't know who owns it now. All I know is that a lot of people have been *shnooping* about recently.'

'Is it possible that Daniel Casey has bought the land?' we suggested.

'Maybe,' she said. 'But there's no way of knowing.'

For city slickers like us this situation seemed most peculiar: Neighbours in the middle of nowhere, and miles apart, fighting like cat and dog and intensely furtive in the conduct of their affairs. It certainly put paid to our picture book idyll of healthy country folk, mucking in happily together while singing melancholic folk songs. We resolved to go and have a chat with Daniel Casey as soon as the weather permitted. The weather permitted very little in Ireland, so this was not before a few more inches had been lopped of the top of the hill.

Just as the Irish are the butt of English jest, so the Irish make jokes about the Kerrymen. The people of Kerry create their gags about the people from Glencar, and the people of Glencar derive their humour from the Casey family. This was an awesome responsibility to rest on anyone's shoulders, but as we were about to discover, the Caseys had shoulders ample to the task and a way of operating equal to the responsibility.

Daniel Casey was a huge man. Well over six, slightly hunched, feet, with shoulder length hair just beginning to gray. Most interestingly of all, apart from the obligatory pair of Wellingtons, he was not wearing the usual farmer's uniform of dark suit jacket, long sleeved white shirt, pullover and cap. Instead he wore a pair of corduroys and a zip-up anorak and looked like an urban 40-something with an account at *Gap*. He smoked a *fag*. There was never a second when he wasn't puffing noisily on one. Rothmans, B&H, Dunhill, whatever, never a roll-up like the other farmers. He didn't have the time to roll them - a suck in and a blow out. With Daniel there was no subtlety and no visible sign of pleasure. It was a desperate action – get the smoke in and get it out.

To watch this man and his droning, dancing machine working together was pure theatre. The huge machine, with tracks like a tank , jointed arm and reverse bucket was moving as if on stage. The bucket was not only used for scooping earth, it had a whole repertoire of actions. The teeth removed the flora, before the bucket scooped the topsoil. Then a rock was isolated and bumped from its cavity. It all happened in unison with the machine's tracks winding back and forth. Each movement appeared to flow into the next. My favorite part of the show was when the machine was elevated on the bucket and the back ends of the tracks. The tracks then moved together - one backwards, one forwards - and the machine crashed down in a different position. And there sat Daniel Casey in the cab, hands on the levers, fingers on the buttons, feet on the pedals - the music of the machine seeming to guide the motion of his body.

Finally, I caught his attention. While he looked interested enough in me to alight from the cab, it was also obvious that his mind was still on the second movement.

'Hello' he called with a smile, reaching into his pocket to pull out and light up a new fag.

Like most Irish he'd spent many years in London, laboring on the city's building sites, which is where he and his twin brother, Luke, had learnt 'the machines' with such complete command. They'd made some money and returned to the family home in Glencar. Their father had been a well-known sheep farmer in the area, but he had been *'clifted'* several years before – in other words, he'd slipped and fallen to his death in the mountains while tending sheep. It was not an unusual cause of death among those farmers who had rights to graze their sheep on the common land of Macgillycuddy Reeks.

As we were chatting, Daniel's twin brother Luke came down the dirt track in a Range Rover, an exotic car for this area and these people - but then nothing the Caseys did was on a small scale.

At first sight there was no difference between the two identically-twinned brothers. They looked the same, spoke the same (their own version of Kerryspeak that even had the locals baffled), said the same things at the same time (then apologised to each other), puffed the same fags and although their clothes were slightly different, one got the feeling that the next day they might be swapped around.

They told me they'd built the dam and hydro-electric scheme on the top of Mount Carrountoohil. They'd also built the road up to the site, a two kilometer stretch of track that went straight up the side of the mountain at a seemingly impossible angle. They'd laid the half meter diameter steel pipe from the dam to the electricity generating station at the base of the mountain. When they'd finished the construction of the dam, the station and the burying of the pipe, the sluice gates at the top were opened for testing. Only a tiny trickle of water emerged from the bottom, not enough to power a torch battery. The project had cost twelve million Irish punt.

Mr. Fitzpatrick, the owner and developer of the project, called together all the men who'd been employed on the project to "workshop" a solution. The Caseys, together with Colm and Padraig O'Mahony, were there. So was Conal Boon, and even Finbar Feneran had taken unaccustomed time out of the pub to put in his three pennies worth.

The problem had to be a blockage in the pipe. The only cheap way to establish its whereabouts without removing two kilometers of buried pipeline was to send someone up it. There was much debate about how this could be done. An opening would have to be made at the bottom of the pipe before it entered the generating station. A rope would be attached to the leg of a volunteer, who would crawl up the pipe with a torch to establish what and where the obstacle might be. Both Daniel and Luke wanted to be the volunteer, even though they were the largest of the people who had worked on the project and could only just fit into its tunnel. But there were no other takers, and after much haggling, it was decided that Luke would do the job, and that Daniel would man the rope.

Mr. Fitzpatrick, was in a state of high agitation. Twelve million fecking punt to power a battery, he kept muttering, when between them all, no-one could produce a working torch. A resentful Mr. Fitzpatrick was persuaded to outlay still more capital in the stalled project by the purchase of a new torch, which he sent down to the town's hardware store for.

Luke took off his wellingtons, revealing a pair of moth-eaten socks half stuck to his feet. On another occasion, the horrible sight might have provoked a communal ribbing, but thanks to the gravity of the situation (and the likelihood that most of the others' footwear was in a similar condition), the assembled party kept their thoughts to themselves as Luke peeled them off. The rope was tied to Daniel's leg above the ankle, and armed with the new torch, Luke shivered his shoulders and then the rest of his body into the pipe. It wasn't long before his feet could no longer be seen. Fortunately claustrophobia was not a word in a man from Glencar's dictionary.

The signals that could be transmitted down the rope were quite basic. Consequently, the plans for Luke's evacuation from the pipe were frighteningly simple. If the rope jerked lightly, Luke had something to report and should be hauled back out. If the rope jerked violently, he should be pulled out fast. If the rope stopped all movement, he should be pulled out very fast.

Probably ten meters of rope had disappeared up the pipe when those at the base started debating what constituted a jerking of the rope. Of course, each time Luke inched forwards his leg would jerk the rope. Was this a signal to say he was in trouble? To complicate matters, after a few jerks the rope would stop moving altogether. Was he in trouble? Was he taking a breather from the difficult leopard crawl up that pipe? Daniel wanted to pull his brother out immediately, but Mr.Fitzpatrick, mindful of his spiraling investment, insisted that Luke was all right. At fifty meters, the tension on the rope changed and became sluggish. Was it because of the length of the rope up the pipe? Or was Luke suffocating to death? Daniel could stand it no more. Against stiff opposition from Mr.Fitzgerald who at one point started his own tug-of-war with Daniel on the rope, he put the rope around his shoulder and charged fifty meters down the hill. Luke came flying out of the pipe, bellowing like a cow in the queue at the abattoir. Daniel came flying back up the hill convinced his brother was seriously injured and tried to embrace him. Luke, still hollering, rejected this affectionate concern with a violent shove. General mayhem ensued with everyone shouting and pushing and Finbar Feneran shouting the loudest....'let's go and have a pint'.

There were several more failed attempts before the problem of the blockage was solved. Luke was pulled unwillingly out of the pipe on a couple more occasions for various reasons, once because the length of rope ran out. Eventually, a huge boulder was found to be wedged where the pipe had to make a slight bend. Naturally, there was much speculation about how it got there, but the general consensus was that during the construction period someone had gone up that hill in the dead of night and dropped the rock down the pipe in a deliberate act of sabotage. Some names and possible motives were mentioned - men who hadn't been employed on the project, neighbours who might have argued that they hadn't been properly compensated for being forced to allow the pipe to be buried on their land. But of course nothing could be proved, even though Finbar Feneran then recalled some idle chit-chat in the pub about "taking action" against the dam project.

Luke, having established the whereabouts and cause of the problem then handed over to Daniel who disappeared up the pipe with hammer and chisel. He chipped away until the boulder was freed up enough to fairly push him out. He emerged with a half meter by half meter rock on his head, to the cheers of the boyos at the bottom and the ecstasy of Mr.Fitzpatrick. Then a squabble broke out between Mr.Fitzpatrick and the lads over who should be paid for the day's difficult, dangerous and project-saving work ... and how much. Mr. Fitzpatrick did not want to part with anything at all, contending that it was not his fault there was a rock in the pipe and insisting that he never asked that a pipe be laid with a rock in it. When he could see that this argument for non-payment was about to provoke violence and probably some other form of guerrilla action, he unwillingly agreed to pay - on condition that he was given a demonstration of the water's unimpeded progress along the pipe. The deal was done.

That was the story the brothers Casey told me while standing out there on the disappearing hill in a constant drizzle of rain, verified and embellished shortly thereafter by Biddy, and later by the other participants that we came to know.

So we're standing on the top of the hill in the grey rain, Daniel, Luke and I, talking about the dam, the pipe, London, this and that. Eventually I could contain my question no longer. One could never ask 'what ARE you doing with your earthmoving on top of this hill' - the question was too direct. One had to ask 'what MIGHT you be doing'. The question then leaves a get out clause: 'I might...but then again I might not...'

'Well' he says, now looking longingly at his idling machine, 'I'm taking away this hill.'

He said it with such seriousness, and with such a sense of the obvious that to probe any further would, I felt, have been grossly insensitive. Adjudging myself an impartial assessor of these earthworks, I could only conclude that every inch removed from the top of that hill exposed the house to greater ferocity from the storm. No matter, I bid them farewell, carrying away my curiosity and their promise that we would soon meet for a pint.

One day, weeks later, the machines stopped, but only for the time it took for Daniel and Luke to disappear in the Land Rover and return towing a huge generator, attached to which was the largest pneumatic drill I'd ever seen. In a moment, Luke was atop the largest rock, now standing exposed and lonely on the bare land, and drilling into the core. After peppering that rock with deep holes, he moved on and did the same thing to the next one. Luke now drilled as Daniel had moved soil and rock - day and night.

A week later he disappeared for the morning. He later told me that thanks to the continuous drilling, he'd developed a headache. But he drilled on and on, until the headache got so bad he was vomiting and couldn't eat. Still he drilled, until one morning he thought he was going to die. So he went to Doctor Billie (so called affectionately as he was regarded as 'the people's doctor') in Killorglin, who refused to give him any pills, but gave him a pain killing shot in the backside and strict instructions to get straight to the hospital in Tralee. Unwillingly Luke drove across the mountain, for he now had a sore bum as well as a sore head. At the Tralee General, they poked him and prodded him, they X-rayed him and asked nosey, irrelevant questions like what was his name and age. Two hours later he still had the headache and had lost most of a morning's drilling. Clearly, the medical fraternity was unable to assist, so Luke administered his own treatment. He went back to the drill and got on with the business of 'blashting that fecking pain right out of my head'. Another week later the holes were drilled and the headache was gone.

Daniel, meanwhile, had filled in the paperwork and made the necessary purchases for the blowing-up of the rocks. Ireland being what it is, one can't simply walk into a store and buy dynamite. But, Ireland being what it is, one can fill out the paperwork and make the necessary arrangements for blowing up rocks.

The day arrived when the rocks were suitably exposed and drilled. The dynamite was escorted by the local guards (whose presence was required to make sure the dynamite was indeed used for blowing up rocks) from Killorglin. An expert was hired to set the right charges in the right way. The rocks and their explosive load were then covered with rubber matting and car tyres, and everyone withdrew the requisite five hundred metres. The detonator box was plunged. There was an almighty bang which we not only heard, but saw and felt from within Lakeview House, as rock fragments flew into the sky, a few small chips landing on the house breaking roof tiles and cracking glass. This latest glitch served to deepen the 'dishpute' between our landlady Biddy, Big Joe and the Caseys.

Over the next days the rock fragments were cleaned up. Then the machine began spreading topsoil from the huge pile that had been created in the beginning. The bare, gravelly earth was neatly covered with a layer of brown topsoil. The top of the hill had indeed been reduced by a couple of metres. The machines were removed and six months later the gorse and other flora had grown over the shrunken hill.

****

Daniel and Luke had another brother, Mathew. The naming of the boys showed a loyalty to Catholicism which was excessive even by County Kerry standards. This family, unlike most other locals were not even regular attendants at Mass. While Catholic philosophy still dominated the ideals of local inhabitants, the institution of the Church was despised behind closed doors. The previous generation had feared the Church. But there'd been simply too many scandals involving the clergy, too many wayward 'fathers' taking advantage of their flock's utter subservience to the Church. For the present generation, fear had been largely replaced by disdain.

Mathew had inherited the family land another two miles in from where we had been standing on the shrinking hill. He was a sheep farmer, married with three young children, the most recent of whom was just a few months old. One day I took a ride as far as one could travel along this track that went past Daniel and Luke's 'hill', into the lands of Derrynafeana behind Coose Lake. At the end of the track stood a clump of fir trees in the middle of which was the ruin of a stone farmhouse, now used for the gathering of sheep. Alongside this farmhouse was a small caravan, with the large window at the front end broken out and covered, not very effectively, by a flapping sheet of plastic. Between the caravan and the old house was a rope washline, strung with children's clothes even though it was, as usual, raining. And consistent with the duality of rain and sheep, there was knee deep mud everywhere.

I had been 'shnooping around', as Biddy would have described it, on account of my interest in old stone cottages. Whenever I could find an excuse for taking off in the car to the end of some lonely track in search of a broken down stone cottage I would do so. Not only did I find the investigation inspirational for the rebuilding of our own house, but I also had in mind making a business in the future of acquiring and rebuilding other cottages.

At the time of my visit I saw nobody, though I experienced a keen sense that my presence was closely observed. This was Mathew and his family's house. In winter the snow lay thick on the ground when the rain was not pelting down. In summer, the rain and the wind howled, and Mathew, his wife and three baby children lived in that caravan without a window, surrounded by the mud and the sheep.

Across the valley Mathew had just completed building the biggest steel framed barn in the district. Here he stored dry bales of hay and feed nuts (high energy) for the cows and sheep. And Mathew drove a black Mercedes Benz. Daniel and Luke had gone up to Dublin to an auction of redundant government vehicles and the one that caught their eye was the Minister of Foreign Affairs' recently discarded Merc. I remember the day that Mercedes – spotlessly gleaming - drove up the valley to Glencar for the first time with the valley folk gawping and gasping at those 'fecking barmy Caseys. Who do they think they are, driving the minister's car? And they didn't even support Fine Gael!" Fine Gael was the party of Government whose minister had just taken delivery of a new car.

Two weeks later there was more gawping and gasping when Mathew Casey was observed driving the Minister's car to market with some bales of hay lashed in the boot, five sheep squashed in the back and two tied into the passengers seat. Mathew, the man with straw in his hair, who kept his wife and three children in a caravan with no window, driving the sheep to town on the leather upholstery of a Minister's Mercedes.

While the Casey's lifestyle was undoubtedly a yardstick by which behavior was measured for entertainment value, very few of these eccentricities made it into the valley's annals of folklore. Of course the story would do the pub rounds for a few weeks, but it was never long before it was superseded by another, fresher yarn. While the Casey's peculiar activities were simply gob-smacking for us new inhabitants, for the locals it was a diet that had already been feasted on forever and showed no signs of letting up. But before moving to the next item on the gossip agenda, the Casey's stories would at least crack the audience's respectful nod: 'Mad feckers ... not a piece of polony for the full sandwich between them.'

4 EVERYONE GOES NUTS EXCEPT ME

The day after our arrival we made the trip down the valley, into the lands of Dromleagh and up the private lane through three gates to our cottage. It was a traditional three-roomed stone building with an addition tacked onto the back. This rear extension was completely overgrown with briar, and a large silver birch grew out of one gable wall. The roof of the main house, while needing to be replaced, had still managed to contain the water, allowing the stone walls to remain solidly intact. There were a number of other stone structures, which had once been used to store turf and log, and as shelters for farm animals - the dogs, goats, hens and roosters. All were now tumble-down and covered in creepers.

The property was on a slope, part of which had been removed (no doubt by hand) and filled in on the lower side to make a level platform on which the house had been built one hundred years earlier. The boundary walls had mostly crumbled over the years of disuse and neglect. On the plus side, there was enough stone around to construct anything, provided one had the spine for it. The cottage itself had been used, since the death of its last inhabitant thirty years earlier, for the penning, counting, marking and shearing of sheep, necessitating the removal of a solid foot of sheep shit before the state and nature of the flooring could be ascertained. In short, there was a huge amount of work to be done just to unearth what was there, let alone start building what wasn't there.

The day was gray and murky, with the rain just about holding off.

Clare and I tramped around the site in our Wellies with baby Ciaran sitting up in a backpack. The ground around the cottage was thick with spiky stinging nettles and scrappy patches of sheep-chewed grass. It was hugely exciting to be about to uncover the remnants of a dwelling, and restore it, in the process creating a home out of this bit of land and pile of rocks. The view, even in this dull light, was awesome. The valley rose up behind the cottage to the peaks of Carrountoohil, and down across the lands around Killorglin and the Slieve Mish mountains. The air was heavy with the mystery of abandonment, the silence gently overlaid by the steady hiss of water over rocks in the river further down the valley.

I wanted to get started straight away and couldn't contain my excitement at the prospect. Clare was not quite so enthusiastic.

'So when you're down here working on the house, what am I to do?'

I tried to be positive: 'You can do a bit of painting, or you can come down here with me.' Clare was interested in fine art. The pressures of living in London with mortgages and jobs meant that she had found very little time to practice what for her was a very important pastime. Our move to the country in Ireland was partly an attempt to provide more time and space for this major interest.

'I don't think I'll get much chance with Ciaran around my feet, but let's see how it goes' she said, also trying to be positive.

So began a pattern which saw me disappearing in the mornings 'to work' and Clare remaining behind at Lakeview House, to look after Ciaran and otherwise attempt to amuse herself. She was unable to travel anywhere as we had only one car.

For me going to 'work' every day was an absolute pleasure. On the way I would decide what could be done, depending on set priorities and climatic conditions. No matter how foul the weather, there were tasks that could be executed. If a howling gale was blowing down the valley, I would work inside: stripping the walls, laying pipes for central heating, re-wiring for electricity, making window frames, re-pointing the stonewalls, building a new cast iron stove, rubbing down and treating the ancient roof timbers.

And on days when the weather allowed, I was outside. There was so much to do, and for each task one had to engage in an entire range of activities. To rebuild the stone wall to the kitchen, first the briar growth had to be peeled off and pulled out, revealing the remnants of a wall and a heap of rubble. I would retrieve the stones from the rubble, then start re-constructing, carefully matching the style of the original stonework. I discovered that almost every wall was built differently depending on the type and shape of the rock, and the temperament of the builder. There were some fundamental rules about knitting the internal and external skins together, of 'laying' the rocks in such a way that if water did get in it would tend to run out when it hit a rock. I discovered that traditional methods of building the stone walls that traversed the local countryside were even more sophisticated, being designed to make the walls impervious to the actions of weather, sheep and cows. Obviously they were highly successful because fifty, one hundred, one hundred and fifty years later, they still stood as built on day one.

Because I was working alone, I also had to work out how to lift huge, heavy rocks above head height. I constructed a series of ramps, up which big stones, substantially heavier than myself, could be rolled using levers. It was backbreaking, though exhilarating work.

Frequently I would come across some fascinating relic of the past. Below the rubble I found bits of steel, a horse stirrup, a cast iron kettle, many tongs and cooking utensils and, bizarrely, a knuckle duster. There were horse-shoes all over the place. On the top of a stone wall coated by a protective layer of soft, green moss, I found a collection of delicately shaped, coloured glass bottles. The inside of the cottage slowly filled up with items which hinted irresistibly at the lives that must have been lived there.

I used traditional materials where possible and practical. I bagged the walls in lime into which I had put a natural colour pigment. I left raw stonework as was, just re-pointing the joints. I replaced the wooden slatted ceiling with old boards I found lying about. I renovated the fireplaces and chimneys, sweeping out ancient soot and grime and replacing dislodged stonework. Windows were remade in the old style. Every task was executed with hand tools as there was no electricity.

I would arrive for work in the morning, and in that country silence and solitude, decide what I felt like doing. Should I retrieve some rocks, or dig the hard shale hole of the septic tank? Did I feel like the sweaty toil of lifting buckets of concrete one by one up ladders to the roof, or should I put together the water supply system to the cottage? I staked and fenced the property to keep the sheep from eating every new shoot or sapling in the garden, planted and nurtured young trees as protection against the wind, rebuilt the boundary wall where it had disintegrated, and laid drainage pipes to stop the never-ending torrent of water that fell from the skies from drowning us all. What I did depended on my mood. There was never an interruption or a disturbance or the irritation of having to accommodate anyone else's needs or temperament. And as the weeks and months went by, out of the rubble and nettles and sheep shit, a house was reclaimed; a home built.

And every day I drove back to Lakeview House, Clare was in a worse state. As much as my existence was about peaceful fulfillment, hers was about excruciating loneliness, boredom and frustration. Her life was lived in an ugly concrete bungalow, for all its gorgeous views of mountain and lake. The almost permanently abysmal weather and baby Ciaran kept her indoors. She would see another human perhaps briefly once a day, and that other human was so unlike herself there was no empathetic peg on which to hang a moan or a complaint about the place or her existence. Anything less than unequivocal expressions of love and admiration for all things County Kerry, tended to be taken as personal insults by the locals.

Even trying to take a walk with the baby was seldom possible. Two hundred yards up the track with the push-chair, the chances were they'd get caught in a fresh downpour from which they'd be forced to seek refuge under a tree for an hour before it eased up enough to dash back to the house.

Clare wanted to paint, but paint what? Paint how? Painterly thoughts hardly had time to percolate before the baby would howl or need feeding. Ciaran's needs also mitigated against her reading a book. There was no TV, only the sound of the wind and the rain in that house with brown walls sweating water down past the Jesus poster haloed by the little electric light that never went off.

In my state of contentment, I didn't realise the extent of Clare's anguish. She never spoke about how she felt – her selfless attempt to play the happy camper was persuasive – instead her dissatisfaction was obliquely expressed. One day she showed me an article in a local newspaper about a woman who had moved from big city England to County Clare several years earlier. She was an artist, and she had decided to return to England, explaining that 'one cannot live on views alone.' As Clare was describing the sentiments expressed by this person with whom she immediately empathized, I was looking out the front windows over the lake. It was late afternoon, the sky above was almost black, but the sun to the west was now lower than the clouds, making the landscape and mirrored lake bright with reflected light. The effect of black sky and sunshine was quite overwhelming. Our view at that moment seemed to mock the idea that 'one cannot live on views alone'. My reaction to the sentiments expressed in the article was almost as unsympathetic as the locals' would have been. From then on, Clare really started to fall apart.

One day I returned home to find her quite clearly on the verge of a serious breakdown. I was shocked, upset, and I had no idea what to do. Going back to England was impossible. But perhaps it would help Clare to be mobile, to be able to get herself to town so that she might meet people she'd have more in common with. There was a time when she would have driven the large van that I used, but her road confidence had evaporated in the face of these narrow country lanes. At the very least, she had to have a car.

Tommy Boon was the youngest of the seven Boon children. We met him when we had first visited Ireland six years earlier, and bought our cottage. Tommy was eleven at the time, and during our visit to his parents, Biddy and Big Joe, he had sprawled across the blue, gloss painted settle in the dark and dingy main room, and tried to smile in a way that did not reveal a missing front tooth. He spoke little, though he occasionally smiled – behind his embarrassed hand. He had given up school two years earlier, and the few erratic classroom years he did have under his pre-adolescent belt, were not sufficient to have taught him to read and write. He spent his time helping around the farm (which he felt was beneath his station) or, more passionately, 'at the cars' with his brother Eoin. When Eoin moved to London, Tommy had little to do, being too small for people to take him seriously as a mechanic.

Two years later, at the age of thirteen, Tommy followed Eoin (and indeed the rest of his brothers and sisters) to London. He immediately found employment on construction sites as a labourer where he joined the rest of the Irish building brigade. In between labouring on sites, he worked with brother Eoin 'on the cars'. They rented rooms in a terraced row in Kilburn and worked on the cars in the street out front. Road widths and car numbers being what they are in London, only one car could pass down the road one way at a time. One day while working underneath a car, Tommy and Eoin left the driver's door open. The first car that wanted to pass hooted for them to close it. Annoyed at having to emerge from beneath the chassis, they were further incensed to see that the two occupants of the hooting car were black. They begrudgingly closed the door, then sent the car on its way with a swearing and a cussing. Some fifty meters down the road the car stopped and the occupants got out. Tommy and Eoin picked up a wrench and a piece of pipe, and took off down the road to teach those 'fecking niggers' an old fashioned Irish lesson. However, they performed a rapid about-turn when the fecking niggers were seen to be just as eagerly approaching, one with an eighteen-inch hunting knife, the other with a meat cleaver. To Eoin and Tommy, this preference for blade over bludgeon represented further proof of the barbaric nature of blacks. The Irish may see themselves as the blacks of Europe, but God forbid, not the niggers.

Tommy had looked us up in London, and I'd spent an evening in the pub with him. He was fourteen at the time, fourteen going on forty. He was living hard. He had grown up fast, proud and happy. For him childhood had been a pain in the butt, a boring waiting game. He was born to be an adult. He smiled broadly. The gap between his teeth had been filled. He had a new confidence and demeanor, all no doubt born out the independence of earning a wage which could afford him such luxuries as a dentist. He didn't need to learn anything to become an adult. Life was about observation and experience, busking in the interim and then making a plan. Although he was illiterate and innumerate, he recognised the colour of notes and the shapes of coins and Tommy paid for pints and got his change just the same as anyone else. He made some money in London and was back in Kerry five years later at the age of eighteen. He arrived back at the family home under Carrountoohil shortly after we had landed.

And so when Clare and I decided to stretch our meagre resources to acquiring an old banger, I solicited the assistance of Tommy, whom I assumed would know the front from the back of such a car, to buy one for us. Together we visited a few second hand car yards. 'Second hand' was too complimentary an epithet to attach to the vehicles we saw. They were fifth or sixth hand, and left in places where brambles or pumpkins had to be removed off of them, before an inspection could be held. Then it was, 'if you're interested, I'll git it going by tomorra.'

Tommy eventually ferreted out a mustard Volvo automatic, one of those cars that works like an electric sewing machine. The grease monkey cum farmer whose premises we were on, told us to return the next day - to give him time to dislodge the chickens from their home on the back seat - and I went home delighted, to tell Clare that our problems were over.

The following day the car was 'going' and barely recognisable, having been cleaned up as well. I got behind the wheel and drove back home into the mountains. There were all manner of strange noises emanating from under the bonnet, not to mention blue smoke, scratchy brakes and pulling wheels, but Tommy assured me that the car was 'sound', not perfect, but 'sound'. And any car that was basically sound only required tinkering to make it 'grand'. He assured me he was well qualified to turn this sound car into a grand one. At the end of the day Clare would have a grand car for the price of a sound one, Tommy would have some employment, I could go back to work on the cottage and all our lives would have benefited.

Tommy did spend a couple of days tinkering about under the hood. When he had completed his work, the car seemed little changed. It now came with a whole series of ground rules. One had to pull out the choke, juggle the gear lever, and press the accelerator twice to the floor before turning the ignition key to get it started. Any deviation from this procedure meant no start. When one pressed the brakes, they required two little pumps first before being effective, and sometimes even then one had to be ready with the handbrake. The reverse lights came on instead of the brake lights, which had a disappearing effect on any car following in the rear. But these were just the little quirks of a banger that never quite made it out of the 'sound' category and into the 'grand', as promised by Tommy.

Anyhow, such faults were as nothing as compared to some of the vehicles I saw on those country roads. Once I observed a neighbour flying by in his Ford Escort without a driver's door. The following week I saw the same neighbour flying by, still without the door, but now without a seat as well. He was sitting on a little wooden box.

****

The next stop was Killarney to get insurance on the Volvo. I had procured the name of a Mr. O'Kelly, who, I was assured, organised insurance for all the locals. As I ascended the dark, creaking steps to Mr. O'Kelly's first floor office, I realised I'd been here before. The offices were directly above those of Mr. O'Connor the attorney. So old was the nameplate on Mr. O'Kelly's door, that I began to wonder how old the notion and practice of 'insurance' actually was, especially round these parts. I pushed open the door and a bell gonged. I was trapped hard up against a counter, the rest of the room consisting of floor to ceiling shelves piled with brown files in a state of some disarray. In the middle of the room stood two desks, one behind the other, both piled high with papers, identical to Mr. O'Connor's office. A young woman made her way through the mess to the counter while an old man whom I assumed to be Mr. O'Kelly, sat almost buried at the back desk reading some papers through thick tortoise shell glasses.

'Good morning,' she said sweetly, ' Can I help you?'

'Yes,' I said, ' I want to inquire about insurance for a car?'
'What insurance?' Mr. O'Kelly shouted from the back. She smiled at me, wordlessly managing to communicate the message that she and I were 'okay', he was nuts. Given that she didn't know me from a bar of soap, she was risking the possibility that I might be like him, and she was nuts.

'I'm not sure,' I said, 'you know, like fire or theft … uh …third party? Uh … like insurance.' I said, beginning to think insurance might indeed be something different in Ireland.
'How old are you?' Mr. O'Kelly bellowed over the fruitless attempt of his assistant to assist me in this matter.

'Thirty –five.'
'How many years have you been driving?' He then proceeded with the usual insurance type questionnaire. Thankfully, Irish insurance wasn't a different thing after all. The girl simply stood between us, smiling at me mischievously.

Finally the questions dried up and he picked up the phone. The person on the other end, asked the same questions Mr. O'Kelly had just asked me. Only this time Mr. O'Kelly answered. When he was asked a question he hadn't asked me, he simply made up the answer. At one point it was clear that the person on the phone had asked about the state of my eyesight, for without hesitation Mr. O' Kelly barked, 'excellent of course, I'm looking at him right now.'

The girl gagged with suppressed laughter, obviously she'd obviously been there before. This time I smiled too. She had been right all along: we were okay, he was nuts.

The insurance disk was stuck to the windscreen, the keys of the mustard Volvo were handed over to Clare, the customised instructions repeated and off she rattled to test the car up the lane behind the house. She was back in the saddle and feeling confident.

When the weekend rolled around, she announced that she would go down to Killorglin on her own and buy the Sunday papers. This bold journey would mark Clare's first separation from baby Ciaran since his birth a year earlier. Not even the driving rain dampened her enthusiasm. She donned all the rain gear, made a dash for the car, and soon the lights lost their focus in the rain, disappearing in the direction of Killorglin.

On her return journey, the little red 'low oil' light blinked on. Clare noticed the light, but given the quirky nature of the car, she ignored it. A short while later, the car blew up, leaving Clare at the side of the road in the pouring rain, weeping her eyes out.

And who should pick her up but Tommy Boon himself, returning from church. Whatever charitable instincts Tommy had polished up during the Sunday sermon, evaporated in the face of Clare's car disaster. 'Don't you know what that red light means, you stupid woman!' he snarled, 'Now you've seized your car.' By the time Tommy dropped her off at home, Clare was in a worse state than before.

I spent the next week fixing the car myself with the help of a

'Haynes' manual, without disappearing every day 'to work'. It eased Clare's loneliness, and gave me a chance to spend some time with Ciaran, taking the pressure off her. I managed to get the car going, but I knew that unless we were able to move into our own cottage very soon, the consequences might be too horrible to contemplate.

5. TILTING AT WINDMILLS

Our cottage was the only house, barring a couple of old ruins, on the west side of the valley looking north-east. Rising up the mountain behind it was our hard-won water pipe, stretching some seven hundred meters up the mountain to a spring just below a sheer face of rock, the top of which announced the summit. Besides the business of constantly monitoring both the pipe against damage by animal hoof or fire (the farmers were constantly trying to burn outcrops of gorse), and the spring where a mouse might have drowned, contaminating our pristine mountain water, it was a wonderful walk with every ascending step revealing new vistas across the valley. On a good day, the Slieve Mish Mountains of the Dingle peninsula fifteen miles away, were visible.

When we purchased the property from Jack and Peig Mullane, we made it a condition of sale that water would be piped from a spring to the house. The Mullane's son, Ger, knew that this spring existed, but wanting to save the cost of the pipe and suspecting that water may be nearer, he called in a diviner. The diviner duly arrived with his cleft stick, and it wasn't long before he was being pulled this way and that by the gyrating prong. He found the water - coincidentally just where Ger suggested he should find it - all of fifty meters from the back fence of the cottage lands.

A delighted Ger called in the dig-o-maniac twins, Daniel and Luke Casey, and their famous earth-moving equipment. A few hours later a three-meter hole was dug. The deeper they went the drier the earth became. Ger called a halt to the digging and summonsed the diviner back. The diviner said that they had dug in the wrong place.

Ger was unhappy with this finding, but the whole process was too advanced to call a halt now. The first hole was filled in, the machinery moved to the new spot, not far from the first, and hole number two was dug. As before, the deeper they dug, the drier the earth became. Ger was furious. This was now costing a lot of money. The diviner had already had his bit, and the Casey's earth moving charges were mounting. Reluctantly, the diviner returned a third time. He and Ger scrambled down into the hole with the stick. At the bottom of the hole the stick was dancing wildly, causing the diviner to conclude that the hole was not deep enough. Daniel boarded his machine and scraped another meter of earth out, until the machine could not go any lower. Not a drop of water sprung. If possible the earth was drier still.

The Casey twins exacerbated an already tense situation by announcing that in all their vast experience in England and Ireland they had never seen such dry earth. Ger was beside himself, demanding his money back from the diviner. The diviner told him to dig deeper. Ger grabbed the divining rod and tried to break it, but it simply bent double clearly sensing the boiling liquids in Ger's own body. The diviner took off down the hill, Ger close behind, slashing at him with the pronged stick. Only when the stick finally broke did Ger give up the chase. The boys filled in the second hole, and Ger laid a seven hundred meter pipe to the spring at the top of the mountain.

My walk up the mountain that day had a purpose. The question of how to get electricity to the cottage had occupied my mind for several years, long predating our arrival in Ireland. While still in England I had visited Machynlleth in Wales, the original home of all technology green and alternative. I had seen the windmills and the photo-voltaic cells powering banks of special batteries. I had even visited an engineer in Oxfordshire who had designed and supplied a 'green' system for a particular application. He required information from me, like average hours of sunlight and average wind-speeds down the valley, none of which I was in a position to supply. Still, I found the notion of living in the Irish backwoods, looking to the elements to supply the necessities of life in complete eco-friendliness, terribly romantic.

The process of renovating the cottage was now three months old, and had reached the stage where unless a decision was made about how the place was to be powered, further progress would be problematic and our moving in date seriously delayed.

I had tried to discuss this matter with Clare.

'How are we going to get electricity down there?' she asked in a very un eco-friendly way. Eco-friendly people are never as direct and uncompromising; they are democratic.

'I'm not sure, but I'm checking out the wind and the sun." Even to my receptive ear, this sounded a trifle imprecise.

'Well there's a hell of a lot of wind, and no sun." she said, "So let's discount the sun. Now how is the wind going to give us hot water so that I can wash the baby's nappies?"

This last question could have been shot down in a hail of humour, but sensibly I resisted.

"For hot water we can burn the turf,' I said, 'but for the lights and the fridge, we need the windmill.'

'What happens when there's no wind' she asked.

'Well, then we've got batteries that have been charged by the wind when it is blowing."

'And what happens if the wind doesn't blow for a week.'

'It never stops blowing,"

'But just say it stops for a week, then all the stuff goes off in the fridge and we have no lights."

'Look, it is possible, I suppose. But then we can get an emergency generator, just in case." This represented the introduction of yet another element not on the original list. Clare delivered the coup de grace: "How much is all this going to cost?"

'I don't know,' I said lamely, 'that's why I have to check it all out.'

Clare spoke slowly, as if giving instructions to a young child: 'We've moved to Ireland, we haven't got a house to live in, we don't know how we're going to make a living, we've got a baby and hardly any money, and you're going off looking at windmills … Why don't you just get power to the cottage?' That was fairly much the end of that. If our romance were to continue, eco-affairs would have to be postponed. I wouldn't tell her that in my head it was only a postponement.

Now I was sitting on top of the mountain wondering how to get power from the Electricity Supply Board (ESB) to our house. I noticed that the power lines came down from the top of the valley above the line of the road. They suddenly changed direction at a particular stone wall, turning ninety degrees down to the bottom of the valley. For a short way, they followed the course of the river, but then turned another ninety degrees back up the slope to resume their original course, above the road. This looked most peculiar to me, and I made a mental note of the phenomenon. As it happened, it looked very convenient for us. Where it turned up from the river it was only some five hundred meters from our cottage, which meant if we had to pay for poles, it would only be two or three to the house.

I went straight to Biddy and Big Joe, to plot our next move. As usual, their advice was not to proceed in the normal way (which would have been to visit the ESB offices and put in an application) but rather to contact Mikey Coffey, whose brother had a friend who put in the poles for the ESB, and he would put us right. I contacted Mikey Coffey, who contacted his brother, who brought his friend to see us. He brought some forms, he checked the house, we paid the bill and a week later the poles were going in and another week later we had electricity. It was mightily impressive.

I also asked Biddy and Big Joe why the electricity supply lines followed such a peculiar course down the valley. This query brought them to the brink of hysteria. They eventually stopped laughing long enough to tell us the story of Paddy O'Sullivan.

Paddy O'Sullivan owned the property around which the electricity lines so neatly and precisely skirted. Electrification came to the valley only in the 1970s. The valley was surveyed, a route for the lines identified and all the farmers over whose land the electricity was to travel were approached for their permission. All were only too happy to sign up, and receive electrification at long last. All except Paddy O'Sullivan.

At the time he was sixty years old. Married to Maire, and with two children, Brid and Paudy, he was disgusted that the local folk were giving into modernisation. 'What's wrong with the gas light and the candles, what's wrong with the kettle on the open fire' he cried. 'It was good enough for our fathers, and their fathers before them. We've had three meals on the table since the famine through hard work and clean living. Now they want to trap us, to exploit us with their electricity. We'll become soft, and who's going to pay for it? We'll have to sell more sheep and milk, so we'll have to work harder. But we'll be softer. And when we can't pay the bills they'll take the land itself. Just like the English tried, and were repulsed by our heroic forefathers with the help of God. Comrades, we must stand together now, and fight this new enemy.' With such nationalistic pleas, Paddy O' Sullivan attempted to weld the valley folk together to resist the arrival of electricity in the valley.

But to a person, the valley folk shook their heads and called him 'that mad fecker' and grumbled that Paddy O'Sullivan would ruin their chances of watching 'Gaybo' (Gay Byrne) in their own homes instead of having to go down to the pub every Friday night to catch Ireland's national chat-show fix.

Paddy O'Sullivan, whose favourite position was perched high on the mountain from where he could see every corner of his lands, was now looking out for a different enemy. It wasn't the fox, trying to poach a lamb. It wasn't a neighbour lifting up the wire fence and pushing through some sheep for a free meal. It was the Electricity Supply Board. His head rested on his knobbly hands atop his stick. He could spy Paudy and Brid doing the chores, he could even spot his wife – who had died by the time we met the O'Sullivans – as she emerged from the house to wash clothes in the freezing stream or take a kettle of water in for the spuds for tea. He was a small man, with sharp, weather beaten features and staring blue eyes. Sitting up there, in his dark suit pants and flapping jacket, his flat cap supported by two huge ears, he resembled a hawk about to swoop on some small prey.

At first sight of the blue ESB van winding up the road, his eyes would widen then narrow. Then he would be up and bounding down the hill, scrambling over ditches, stick waving with frightening intent. He'd get down to the road just in time to try to stop the van. Before the ESB officials became accustomed to his antics, the van would stop, the innocent driver thinking there had been an accident of some sort. Paddy O"Sullivan would hurl abuse through the window, pushing the knob of his stick into the face of the driver, and then give the van a resounding smack as it took off again at great speed.

The ESB sent local politicians up to see if they could talk sense into Paddy's head. They got half way up the steep slope to his old stone cottage, before they spotted him flying down that mountain like the phoenix. The sight was apparently so scary, that long before Paddy was within striking distance, the politicians had turned tail and were beating a retreat down that hill faster than old Paddy himself. The priests – who were largely sympathetic to Paddy's stand - refused to intervene: Paddy was of the old school, they appreciated his salt of the earthiness, and anyway, all these new-fangled things (and especially TV), had caused a certain straying of their flocks.

When the surveyors arrived with their dumpy levels and theodolites, they had to be accompanied by the guards who did everything short of locking Paddy up to prevent an assault on the technicians. In the end, at huge expense to the ESB, the power supply lines carefully skirted the borders of his land.

"And it wasn't six months later," Biddy continued, 'Paddy O'Sullivan got dressed up in his Sunday best and made the trip to Tralee, something he hadn't done for years, and the offices of the ESB, to ask them if they would give him a little power just for the light in the living room, not for all those other things you understand. They told him to go to hell."

Paddy O'Sullivan was also responsible for the loss of another popular local event. The annual car rally between Killorglin and Waterville used the road through the valley. For the valley folk, the car rally was a big deal. Some did teas for the spectators and made a few bob, some were able to offer good friends grand stand seats, and all the boys older than ten were, like Tommy Boon, into cars. They all had been tinkering with their parents' car and sometimes tractors for years, and some in their early twenties even fancied themselves, souping up a car and entering the rally.

Paddy O'Sullivan couldn't stand the car rally. It was a danger to his animals, and the incoming flood of people was not to be trusted. They stood on his stone walls, knocked over fences and threw litter into his fields. On the day of the rally he would be ready for them, patrolling the road with his stick. And all the young boys would be ready for Paddy O'Sullivan. The game was to bait him until he was blue in the face, flying up and down the road with flailing stick. Many kids would feel that stick across their backs as they tried to make an escape, but that was also part of the fun. On one occasion a rally driver was also introduced to Paddy O'Sullivan.

It was an unfortunate coincidence that where the road passed through his lands it took an almost hairpin bend. One vehicle lost control on the bend and fairly flew over the stone wall below, landing neatly in one of Paddy's fields. In a flash Paddy was there, jumping from the wall onto the roof of the car just as the shaken driver stumbled out of it. The unfortunate driver must have been counting his blessings – he was uninjured – when Paddy's stick came down on his helmeted head. The following year the rally organisers changed the route.

Shortly after moving in to our cottage with electricity, we heard a car coming up the lonely cul-de-sac. A beat-up Ford Escort with bale cord tying the boot down stopped at the gate, and out climbed Paddy O'Sullivan and his son Paudy, dressed in old-style shabby black suits and ties, with caps off and hair brushed. This visit was official. We had not yet met the O'Sullivans, and they had come down to introduce themselves and welcome us as their new neighbors. It was very formal, and there were strict rules of etiquette. Invite the guests in, sit and chat for a while over some hard tack while the wife got a spread on the table. The spread should consist of spuds (obviously home grown), milk, some soda bread and a pot of tea. If one was really trying to show off, a nice bit of boiled bacon would be set on the table. We failed in the food and etiquette departments, and their reaction was similar to that of your average Westerner on being presented with a just hatched boiled bird in Malaysia – concealed horror, incomprehension and embarrassment.

Paddy O'Sullivan had been best friends with the last person to have lived in 'our' cottage. Mikey Mullane had died some thirty years earlier. Paddy described where the pigs were slaughtered and how they were salted and hung up on the beams above where we were sitting; how the sheep and cows lay on straw at floor level, while the adults slept on a platform and kept warm by the rising animal heat. Strangely, the last inhabitants never had children. The woman suffered from the 'nerves'. The 'nerves' was the term for any mental affliction, and in this case it sounded as if she was probably an agoraphobic - she never left the house, and if there was a visitor, she wouldn't come out of the bedroom.

Paddy O'Sullivan also described to me the location of an overgrown graveyard for the valley's unbaptised babies and young children. I subsequently found it on one of my walks, though it was very well hidden, even without the overgrowth and *sally's*. It had such an eerie, sad feeling to it. The idea that children and babies were thrown away in shame and disgrace for dying without baptism, was beyond me.

By the time Paddy and Paudy O'Sullivan left, our house too had an eerie, sad feeling. Every stone now evoked images of toil and graft and the bitter sweat and tears of folk eking out a hopelessly meagre existence. Bizarrely, by re-building the cottage stone by stone, we were engaged in re-establishing some sort of continuum.

Paddy O'Sullivan ran his familial affairs like he did everything else… with his stick. His wife Maire, long dead, had obviously given in and given up. The children, Paudy and Brid, had been shaped to take over. Brid did the household chores - the washing of clothes in the stream, cooking of spuds and sweeping out the cottage. The toilet was a bucket, the bathroom a rock by the stream. The word Spartan comes to mind, but it still describes pure comfort compared with how they lived. When Brid was in her early twenties, Paddy O'Sullivan caught a whiff of rebellion to his frugal, pre-industrial approach to life. Brid emerged from the bedroom wearing a pair of trousers instead of the skirt she had worn since she could walk. Paddy O'Sullivan beat her so badly she did not show her face outside for weeks.

Brid was now forty. Her uniform was a straight blue skirt, white blouse and matching blue cardigan. She always wore stockings and neatly-heeled shoes. Her comfort and companion was a radio. She listened to it in that lonely cottage, her ever-napping head buried in her arms slumped on the table. Brid was an intelligent woman who new lots of things. She kept on saying 'I know' when one was describing South Africa or the difficulties of child rearing. She also suffered the 'nerves'. She was on heavy medication, and Paddy allowed her to go to town once a week – on dole day - to purchase fresh supplies of her medicine. She would be chaperoned by her brother Paudy. Her blue eyes were glazed, shining out hopelessly from huge black rings. Brid had the eyes of a heroin addict.

Paudy was different. With Paddy now eighty years old, Paudy did everything on the farm. Unlike Brid, he accepted Paddy's philosophy and went about his business in contented silence. He didn't want the TV and he expressed no need of home comforts. He planted his shpuds, he tended his shpuds, he dug up his shpuds, he carted his shpuds to the barn, he stored his shpuds, he ate his shpuds. It was the same with the milk, the sheep, the turf and the hens. Whatever he couldn't do or supply himself, he didn't need - simple as that.

We had just replaced the roof on our cottage when Paudy appeared and asked if I could come up and see Paddy about 'a quotation'. I made an appointment and was soon trudging up the steep slope to their cottage across the valley. The dogs announced my arrival and all three O'Sullivans greeted me on the steps of the cottage. After formal welcomes, I looked out over the valley – a magnificent sight from that elevation.

Then I noticed an impressive bank of fuchsias blooming right across the front face of the cottage which obscured the bottom of the valley, save for a section in the middle which had been neatly cut out like a window. The cut-out framed our cottage perfectly on the other side of the valley. Naively I asked why the fuchsias were cut in this way. 'So that we can see you' said Paddy O'Sullivan, without blinking.

I didn't know how to react, but Paddy O'Sullivan carried on.

'The shmoke coming from your chimney looks like you're burning wet logs.' Realising that every move we made, inside and outside the house, was being closely monitored by people who could spot a mouse at a thousand metres, I immediately got paranoid. Was this a reference to the fact that I was collecting wood from lands around the cottage which I shouldn't be doing?

'And I see you're having some difficulty keeping those sheep out your land.' Oh God, was this a reference to the fact that I caught a sheep in our fences eating some young, recently planted trees and beat the shit out of it?

Then he added, to show he was a man of the world and not averse to a little humour...'I saw you take a piss on the road the other day, ha,ha,ha.'

I was shocked into silence, desperately thinking of any other things I might have done that I wouldn't have wanted the locals to see. We went into the cottage. There was an ancient table under the window with four rickety chairs, a traditional Irish bench and an open fireplace sporting a hanging kettle. The floor was raw concrete. I was invited to sit at the table. I looked out the window, and there was our cottage, perfectly framed. I was beset by another little shudder: we were the closest thing the O'Sullivans' had to TV. Once the floury shpuds had been fished out of the kettle and put on the table, we got down to the business of the day.

'Now that you have finished your roof, we want you to put a new roof on for us,' Paddy announced.

I had noticed that their corrugated iron covering was getting very rusty, in fact I was surprised that they didn't have more leaks and said so.

'The old iron is on top of *da tatch,*' said Paddy.

Sure enough, an ancient looking thatch lay beneath the rusty outer roof. I was simply to put new iron on the replace the old. I told them how much I thought it would cost - to me it was such a compliment and breakthrough to be asked to work for one of the locals that I cut my labour cost to the bone. Paddy O'Sullivan was happy with that, the deal was done and as soon as I had procured the material, I made a start on the job.

In the following days I took up my position on the roof, replacing one sheet at a time to avoid being caught by the weather. Paddy O'Sullivan took up his position on a rock from which he could observe my every movement. All was going well until a few days into the job I lost my footing on the oiled surface of the new iron sheets, slipped down the roof and fell off the edge. I landed on my back on the ground, very luckily on a softish patch of moss covered earth. But the wind was knocked out of me, and for a several minutes I lay gasping like a beached fish. Paddy O'Sullivan was up like a fox, darting round in circles holding his head, repeating Hail Mary's over and over. When I finally got to my feet, I went over to him and held him by his two arms – by now he was hysterical. Once he came to his senses and understood that I was alive, he shrieked again in fright and let fly with a heartfelt string of *tanks* ... 'tanks be to God, tanks to the good Lord, tank you Jaysus'.

We went indoors to recover with a pot of tea. After an hour's worth of conversation about how the accident happened, what a miracle it was I was unhurt and Paddy's terrible fright, he confessed that what had concerned him most was the realisation that if something disastrous had happened to me, they would not have shied away from their responsibilities. I looked bemused, so Paddy explained that Paudy would have had to take on Clare and the kids. The idea of me dead, and Clare and the children moving in with Paudy, Paddy and Brid, is a notion that still has the power to wake Clare up in the middle of the night, sweating and slightly delirious.

The purpose of doing the new iron on the O'Sullivan's cottage was twofold. Aside from the fact that the roof needed replacing, it was also the O'Sullivan family's turn to host the annual stations. Every year, one household in the parish was chosen to have a mass said in their house and for the house and family to be blessed. This ritual was controlled by the local priest who enforced it rigorously, as it was a way of bringing in revenue, and keeping in touch with his flock, especially the stragglers.

There was another piece of more practical logic to the event: it was expected that a special effort would be made to get the house looking good and working well for the big occasion. After all, the priest might refuse to bless a shoddy house. For the locals, it was a day off from normal activity, and the household was expected to provide free booze for the guests (the priest usually stayed only as far as the consumption of tea and buns.) So at least one day a year friends and enemies came together, and after the first few drops, old arguments were either forgotten or fuelled.

As we were now included in the locality, we were invited to the O'Sullivan's 'stations'. The concrete floor had been swept for the occasion and they'd borrowed a few chairs, which stood around the perimeter of the room. Once the mass had been said, the tea and ham sandwiches devoured and the priest had left (after eyeing out the newcomers in a way that made me very nervous), out came the bottled Guinness and the whisky. Fifteen or so 'parishioners' remained in their seats making embarrassed small talk to their neighbours or contemplating their glasses in silence. They all knew each other so well, not through normal channels of communication, but by 'spying' on each *a la* the O'Sullivans on us. Yet they had to behave as if they didn't know anything about each other, for fear of being branded nosy. A stony silence ensued. Until Ned The Banker Liddy, a small degenerate looking man who lived directly across the valley from ourselves, and who was infamous for being unable to hold his booze, started his own bit of *craic* in the corner. He was feeding our son Ciaran, who was two years old at the time, a bottle of Guinness. Ciaran took a fancy to the drink, and Ned was only too happy to raise the bottle to his lips and pour in another huge mouthful. He called everyone's attention to this bit of fun, laughing merrily at how Ciaran was beginning to wobble while pouring another draft down his toddler throat. I felt the tension rise in the room. It was clear that everyone had the same thought: would the newcomer, the 'blow-in', take exception to this activity, and if so what will he do?' Should I walk across the room and punch Ned Liddy's stupid head in? This was my preferred course of action, but not the right choice. Clare was looking at me pleadingly. Ciaran was doing an unbalanced little dance in the middle of the room closely watched by everybody, then Ned's voice boomed out: 'Here boy, come and git some more mama's milk' and Ciaran was there with the bottle back in his mouth. The room was silent, expectant. The atmosphere could be cut with a knife.

'Don't give him anymore!' I shouted menacingly across the room.

Ned lowered the bottle, saying 'what harm, what harm'. He wasn't yet drunk enough to take this further, thank goodness. He was also a bit wary of us, the foreigners, and what we might be capable off.

'Ciaran, come here' I ordered. As he stumbled across the room, some of the woman said ' "ah, the poor *cratur.*'

The atmosphere instantly lightened up. I had passed a type of a test, shown that I could be a 'man' if necessary. There were, I was soon to discover, more tests to come.

6. SORTING THE MEN FROM THE RAMS

It wasn't long before I was put through another test to see whether, by the standards of the valley, I qualified as a real man. A man had to be physically strong and fearless; a man wouldn't show emotion; a man was unafraid of muck and shit and blood and pain – one's own or anyone else's. My first test was the animal-blood-pain test, with a bit of physical strength thrown in.

Conal Boon appeared at the front door of Lakeview House one morning calling urgently for my assistance. Did I have a hacksaw? Then bring it, quick.

A sheep was loosely tethered to a steel post in the yard at the back. To city folk, a sheep is a sheep. Sure, one has heard about rams and ewes – the stuff of Grade 3 education. But city slickers – even those who've visited a farm and seen live sheep - would rarely find it necessary to pick out the ram from the ewes. But there is a significant difference. All those green fields one passes at one hundred and twenty kilometers per hour on the highway are the grazing paddocks of ewes or neutered lambs, not rams. Rams are only used for their ability to provide seed, and when reproductive science is advanced enough they will be done away with altogether, because they are wild, dangerous animals.

The sheep tethered to the post was a ram with a huge pair of curled horns, and herein lay the problem. The horn tips had curled over so radically that they had grown into the ram's cheeks. The ram was no longer able to close its jaws, the pain must have been excruciating and the animal was in some distress. The task was obvious – cut off the horns with a hacksaw. Conal and I. There was no-one else about. One to hold, one to cut. And then swop.

'Hold him' Conal instructed in his usual expansive, friendly way.

I sat astride the animal's back and grabbed its neck. Both Conal and the ram shook their heads and looked at me.

'What might you be doing?' Conal asked with genuine curiosity.

With the ram beginning to buck and whoop with the strength of a small horse, Conal told me to get off.

He mounted the ram, sitting on its shoulders with his legs down the side of its neck and his feet spreading the ram's legs. He grabbed the animal under the mouth and wrenched it back until I thought the neck would snap. The ram was blowing foam through its nose and mouth - not so much in pain but in anger.

'Now cut the fecking thing,' Conal barked.

I got in between his arms with the hacksaw and started cutting through the horn which was the width of coffee cup. It was tough going. The thing was bucking and snorting, but Conal kept a firm grip and no matter which way the head was twisted I kept on cutting. Finally one was through, it fell, dangling out of the hole through the ram's cheek.

We had a short break then it was my turn to hold while Conal cut. The ram saw me coming, and save for some deft bobbing and weaving on my part, it would have taken my knee out with a back kick from its sharp hooves. Then I was on its back, over its shoulders and under its jaw with my two hands pulling it up like the prow of a boat on high seas.

Conal took up the cutting, and soon the second horn lay on the gravel. Conal kicked it into a bush for no reason other than to dismiss it as useless rubbish never to be seen again.

My clothes smelt of sheep and shit. My hands were covered in grime, lightly greased with slime. My shoulders ached, but I was happy as I felt my efforts must have been marked at least seven out of ten.

Word got around that I was a bit of a 'boyo', but the jury was still out on whether I had done enough to be raised into full blown manhood. After all, even if I reached this higher station, I didn't have a hope in hell of ascending to the elevated heights of, say, Luke Casey, one half of the mountain-moving Casey twins. But then even in the valley Luke Casey was something special. In his youth he had won the 'strong man' competition at all the local fairs. Each of the small districts had an annual country fair. The locals would show up with a few brushed nags, the travellers would set up a half-baked fairground that would have the small kids charging around with excitement, the local pub would do a bomb, and there was a strong man competition. In the years that we went to the fairs - expectantly, sentimentally - they were always a disappointment: not only were they small and tatty, but they were usually rained-out too. But the strong man competition attracted interest in any weather. There were the old pros like Luke Casey, challenged by the hopefuls, and there were those in it for a laugh, to amuse the crowd. The competition included several tests of strength like pulling a loaded trailer, blowing up a sheep's bladder until it popped and lastly - the highlight - tossing a tree trunk the furthest distance. And Luke Casey won the lot, every year.

Luke once had occasion to put one of these disciplines to good use in real life. Along the *boreen* which dissected his land at Coornameana, the workers from Telecom Eireann arrived with their equipment. At regular intervals they dug holes for telephone poles and cable to another farmhouse further in along the *boreen*. Luke was outraged. What about his view? He didn't want poles and cable rudely interrupting his view of the lake. Until then I don't believe anybody knew or even considered that Luke possessed such strong aesthetic sensibilities. After all, he was a man who had built a road up the highest mountain in Ireland scarring it forever. He had erected some of the biggest barns in the locale on virgin landscapes and was responsible for starting to build three houses the construction of which had been abandoned at window sill height. Now three telephone poles on a plot of empty land ten kilometers from where he lived, were more than he could bear. Luke's aesthetic conversion was doubly mystifying to the valley folk who saw only progress and convenience in cables and poles. Luke paid a visit to the offices of Telecom Eireann in Tralee to complain and demand that the cable be buried, rather than hoisted and hung. Officials were adamant that forms had been sent out, and affected parties had been given ample opportunity to express any objection. Luke had never seen the forms on account of his principle of ripping up any official looking letter, fired by the reasoning that the vast majority of official looking letters were the bearers of bad news, and no news was better than bad news.

He watched from a distance as one by one the poles were hoisted into position by the machine with a steel grab device on its bulky frame. Rocks were then thrown around the base of the pole in the hole, and topped with more filling. After a productive day, the workers packed up their equipment and disappeared homewards for the evening.

No sooner were they out of eyeshot than Luke Casey was at the first pole, inspecting it, sizing it up, his powers of concentration in overdrive thanks to the increased velocity of the puff-puff-puff on his fag. When he was ready, he ripped the fag from his mouth and ground it into the mud. He gave the pole a little nudge with his shoulder, went to the opposite side and rammed into it with his body a bit more firmly. From all angles he hit that pole until it was standing at a slight angle. He moved in close and wrapped his body around it, his legs bent. He took a deep breath and closed his mouth; his cheeks bubbled out like the sheep's bladder at the fair. Luke knew not to try a direct extraction, instead he shivered his body like a dentist quivering his pliers in pursuit of a molar's long roots. The pole moved. He bent his legs again, took another breadth ... and slipped that pole out of its socket. It keeled over, making the sound of falling timber as it crashed onto the rocks at the side of the road.

Luke extracted the other two offending poles the same way. Then he treated himself to an unimpeded gaze at his beloved Lough Acoose.

The following day, the workers arrived and were completely baffled. They could find no evidence of any mechanical device or even of hand tools that might have caused the poles to change their alignment from vertical to horizontal. A gale had ripped across the lake as usual during the night, but surely that was not sufficient to take the poles out? The workers speculated that maybe a combination of the gale and some inadequate wedging and filling around the base had caused the poles to collapse. They put in a report about this strange turn of events, and proceeded to re-erect the poles.

The following day they returned and the same unbelievable scene greeted their popping eyes. The three poles were flattened. It was then that they understood that someone was delivering a very clear message. They decided to proceed with the balance of the thirty poles that were still required to reach their destination, and let the supervisor sort out this problem before attempting to re-erect the fallen poles again.

The supervisor established that the land belonged to the Caseys, and rather than attempt to resolve things through the guards and the law, he decided to tackle the problem directly with the Caseys on his next tour of inspection. When next the supervisor inspected the works at Coornameana, the Caseys were not there so he drove down to the family's house at Gortmaloon. On this particular day Luke and Daniel Casey were digging drainage channels around a boggy field. They spotted the Telecom Eireann supervisor in his large official looking car long before the supervisor spotted them. He looked very official. The boys believed he could be from the tax office, the dole office, the customs police or even a plain clothes guard, so they rapidly alighted from the digger and tractor respectively, and sprinted off across the boggy field in the direction of the rocky hills. The supervisor stopped his car just in time to see the Caseys reach the base of the rocks and begin scrambling into their cover. He knew that he had reached the cause of the problem: he didn't know how or why, only that he'd definitely arrived. The supervisor had encountered the odd behaviour of these mountain types before. He wrote a conciliatory note outlining how he just wanted to talk to them about how to resolve the problem of the poles without blaming anybody, and left it in the cab of the still idling mechanical digger.

The supervisor returned three hours later, and this time he parked his car out of sight and crept up on them in the hope of making it impossible for them to bolt like march hares again. His plan worked perfectly, for the first the boys knew of him was when he popped out from behind a gorse bush very close to where they were operating. They were snared.

The supervisor wisely did not mention the fallen poles but requested that the boys make a suggestion about how the cable might cross their lands. They agreed that burying was probably a better option than hanging, but the boys would have to dig and lay the plastic pipe through which the cable would be pulled, at their own expense. Luke and Daniel readily agreed.

I was nowhere in the same beef league as Luke Casey, and was never going to be. I had struggled a bit with the ram and then I was invited along on a hay bales loading 'outing'. The Boons and the O'Mahonys had bought a couple of fields of hay bales from a farmer some miles away. The cutting and baling had been done, and all that remained was to load the bales aboard the trailers and tractor them back to the farms. Big Joe came as supervisor - his ruined back preventing him from doing any loading. Colm O'Mahony, Conal, small Joe Boon, Thady Mor and myself made up the rest of the loaders.

We arrived with the tractors and trailers as planned. The farmer pointed out which bales had been sold to us. Big Joe introduced me as a blow-in 'all the way from California.'

'California?' asked the farmer, addressing me. I thought big Joe was taking the mickey out of the farmer, so I continued the *craic*.

'Yes, all the way from California,' I said, hoping he wouldn't question me further, and didn't have an ear for accents. He had nothing more to say to me but he continued the chat with big Joe. The farmer looked confused when big Joe said,

'A white man from California.' Then I caught on. Big Joe was not having some craic with his farmer friend. To him there was no difference ... South Wales, South Dakota, South Africa, Soviet Union ... it was all just out there somewhere, and in some cases, here today gone tomorrow. Unlike the valley and the valley folk, who had been there forever, and were not going anywhere.

A pike was handed to each man, and one for me. Conal approached the first pile of hay bales. The trailer was maneuvered into position. He thrust the prongs of the pike into the bale, and in one movement, gracefully whirled it to shoulder height and dropped it on the trailer. I tried the same. I couldn't lift the bale and I realised that all the boys had been waiting for this moment, and now they started to laugh. Conal showed me again how the task had to be executed in one movement using the correct balance of body weight and momentum to swing the heavy bale upwards and onto the trailer. With huge effort I managed one, but then the prongs of the pike did not come out of the bale and I was nearly swung onto the trailer with the bale. The boys laughed again. After a few attempts at spiking and hurling bales I was managing to get them onto the trailer after a fashion, but only by expounding reserves of energy that should have been used to accomplish the proper technique. I became aware that the boys were standing round, chins on their pikes, sniggering and watching. So I stopped and topped the handle of my pike with my chin as well. Then they grudgingly set to work. The pile of bales on the trailer grew higher and higher; the last bales were tossed off the top of the pike well over twelve feet high. It was physical murder, but I was determined to keep up and do my share.

Through the afternoon another important fact of bale loading expertise dawned on me. Some bales were substantially heavier than others. This was because of the moisture in the hay, which varied from bale to bale according to how each had lain in the field. I was learning to recognise the light ones by sight. And I wasn't loading any of them. The boys somehow got those ones first and left the dead weights for me. I said nothing, but I started making sure that I too got to some of the light ones first. The idle banter changed to grunts of effort. Then I noticed that the other side of the trailer was being loaded much slower than my side. On it went through the afternoon and into the darkness of early evening. My body ached. I thought I could hear my joints creaking. Both hands were covered in blisters long since popped, but not a complaint passed my lips, no display of discomfort did my body language speak, only serenity was written on my face.

We boarded the last homeward-bound tractor high up on the bales. We lay up there, pointing for once at a wide and cloudless heaven while the tractor chugged the half an hour back to the farm. It was blissful. The tractor was passing Lakeview House on its way up to the Boon's barn on the hill. Big Joe commanded the driver to stop.

'Fuck off, boy', he ordered me, 'we'll offload at the top, you've done enough.'

Another test had been passed.

THE HOUSE AT THE EDGE OF THE WORLD

7. POACHED SALMON

Occasionally, we visited the Boons, our first Irish friends and landlords, at their old cottage up the steep, hairpin track behind Lakeview House. In these parts, socialising was unusual. Unless there was farming business – inspiring mutually suspicious neighbours to cooperate in sheep shearing or hay loading and share a refreshment together afterwards - the farmer and his family would spend their evenings in isolation. An early '*tay*' would be had, followed by long hours in front of the open fire, mostly in silent contemplation of the flames and glowing turf, until bedtime.

We pounded on the closed dark door of early evening, and heard from behind it Biddy Boon's shrill 'come in', spoken in a tone which said 'we know who you are and that you're coming, so there's no need to knock'. Ducking through the low-slung door frame, we entered the main room of the traditional cottage. Big Joe, lying across the settle looking into the fire, had propped himself up on an elbow as a courtesy to his guests. Tommy Boon was sitting in a tatty armchair on the other side of the fire, while the Boon's daughter Breda, and Biddy were still clearing away the last of the 'tay' things. They were bent over a recently installed steel sink filled with boiled water from the kettle. There was no other running water in the house. The toilet was a long drop in the backyard, or a potty under the bed for especially cold winter evenings. Personal hygiene was attended to courtesy of a bucket.

Clare had been shopping with Biddy two weeks earlier, and they'd both bought some thermal underwear on a special offer at one of the stores. Clare asked Biddy if the thermal description was indeed apt.

Lovely,' said Biddy, 'I've been warm as toast'.

'Mine shrunk a bit in the wash, did you find that?' asked Clare.

'I haven't taken mine off yet, I'll tell you when I do,' replied Biddy, without missing a beat.

Chairs were taken from the table and placed in front of the fire for us and big Joe ordered Tommy to pull out the whisky and glasses.

There followed the usual sequence of precursory chit-chat: 'What a beautiful evening for this time of year, it may be cold but it's clear and there's a bit of a moon peeking through, so maybe it'll be dry now for another day, if we're lucky ...we needed it mind, those last few weeks it was deadly, that howling gale and cold blasht of a storm, it clear knocked the door of the cowshed off its hinges' and the cows, and the new foal...a difficult birth...'had to get the blashted vet up, cost a fortune, the greedy cunt, ...but the poor cratur almost died, and would have taken Blossom with her'.

The recounting of Blossom's difficult birth dislodged another memory of Biddy's - of another cow named Blossom – Blossom II's predecessor in fact.

Big Joe had been herding his cows, led by Blossom I, back from town where every Thursday morning a market was held. The farmers would take some of their stock down to market in Killorglin in the hope of making a sale to a buyer who might be passing through town. It was mid-afternoon on a summer's day on which the sun was actually shining. The usual head of traffic had built up behind the cows blocking the road, and Big Joe was awaiting a widening of the road where he could part the herd and let the traffic through. The first car in the queue was a fancy hired car, boasting a female American tourist behind the wheel and two companions.

Not minding in the least the holdup, the driver had time to contemplate how she might further embellish the essential quaintness of this perfect little Irish vignette. Sticking her head out of the window, she yelled at big Joe in her southern belle drawl......'why are those cows looking so damned unhappy?'

Big Joe loved nothing more than playing the Irish puk for people like this. He bellowed a reply in his deepest Irish mountain brogue, which was completely unintelligible to the Americans, or to anyone else for that matter.

'Could you repeat that?' yelled back the woman, wanting to catch every detail for her next dinner party back home. Still she couldn't hear his reply. But then the road had widened, the dog had manoeuvred the cows out of the path of the cars and the Americans had pulled up real close to big Joe.

'Why are those cows looking so damned unhappy?' the woman said again. Big Joe dropped his Kerry mountain accent and in good English he replied: 'If you had your tits pulled twice a day and got fucked once a year, you'd also look unhappy.'

The tourist's happy holidays expression was wiped from her face. She hastily rolled up her window, and left big Joe and his cows in a gray haze of exhaust fumes.

At that time Biddy did 'teas' at the house. Some rocks on the main road were painted with TEAS and an arrow, and tourists would come up to the house on a nice day for a little refreshment. The American woman certainly needed some refreshment, and swung off the main road as directed by TEAS. A little shaken by her close encounter with a native, but already seeing the anecdotal potential, the tourist proceeded to tell Biddy about the disgusting peasant who'd spoiled their afternoon. Biddy wholeheartedly endorsed the party's outrage. 'Now sit yourselves down, rest those weary legs and forget about some f ... ah, fat peasant down that road.'

By the time the first of big Joe's cows turned into the yard, Biddy and the Americans were having a right jolly old time, fresh tea having been bought and even a second load of 'hang sangwiges', which the Americans didn't really want, but which was their way of rewarding this decent Irish person.

Big Joe removed his wellingtons outside the front door, as was his custom, and marched into his living room. The seven mile walk to town behind a herd of cows, the standing around on the 'square' in town for five hours amongst the pissing and defecating animals, a few jars for lunch and the long walk home had left big Joe a stinking mess with great toes protruding through destroyed socks. He marched into the twinky tea scene and headed for his settle where he lay down with his feet up against the fireplace.

The southern belle shrieked: 'That's the disgusting peasant with the cows I told you about!'

And Biddy replied: 'Disgusting peasant he may be, but he's my husband'. The scene was closed in another haze of exhaust fumes.

Big Joe made a virtue of wearing a particular outfit long past the time when it could easily be fitted to the body. His daily apparel seemed to consist of any old get-up, no matter how torn or decayed, as long as it afforded some protection against the elements. He once emerged wearing a woollen jumper that was so full of holes even to have put it on was an art.

But when big Joe went to the pub he was a changed man. After a thorough scrubbing in the bucket, he'd put on a pressed black suit, sparkling white shirt and shiny black shoes. And he'd shave. Clare had told me that all the women dyed their hair. This procedure was always carried out at home, which meant that mistakes were common. We discovered one day that Biddy dyed big Joe's hair as well. We found out when he popped up one day sporting a pale green thatch. Something had gone wrong, but big Joe wasn't embarrassed about it - as long as no gray was visible he didn't care what it looked like.

We had known the Boons a full six months now. Whenever we spent time together I attempted to coax big Joe into telling stories of his life, a life interesting in its total difference to my own. He was also a remarkable storyteller. They were stories of a people who had lived in the tradition of struggle on a landscape which, barren and uncompromising as it was, still provided food, shelter and a type of security. And in it were the land evictions by English landlords and then their bailiffs, the famine, the Black and Tans, continuous war, the IRA, spies, and politicians. And overlaying it all was the Catholic Church. Sitting round the open hearth the stories came, night after night, year in year out, until they became part of the communal psyche. The stuffing of these tales was often quite mundane, but the way Big Joe told them was pure magic. He wove his few words in ways that seemed to give simple stories a profound wisdom, wisdom which on later reflection was quite illusory. Both these qualities were common in the people of those mountains: they were all great talkers and narrators, and their stories always left the listener uncertain as to whether what one had just heard was genius *a la* Beckett and Joyce, or complete madness.

One unusually clear, bright night, Big Joe began to talk about salmon, and it wasn't long before the conversation turned to salmon poaching. There was the time the Boon family was 'fishing for sport' and they saw the headlights of a guard's car. So Tommy slipped the salmon up the sleeve of his leather jacket and the guards were fooled - except the jacket smelled so bad afterwards that Tommy was never able to wear it again.

Hoping to egg him into more 'fishing for sport' stories, I asked big Joe: 'So how do you catch the salmon?'

Big Joe's response was incredulous: 'Have you never caught a salmon before?"

'No, but I'm happy to see how it's done.' I challenged them.

'Have we still got that old harness you once made?' Big Joe asked Tommy, who went off into the bedroom in search of the exotic implements required for a poaching expedition.

He returned with a leather harness and a car headlight, and disappeared again out the front door and came back some time later with a car battery, a pike and some wire.

Big Joe started explaining how to use these goods. The harness fitted over the shoulder and neck, and supported the car battery at waist level. The car headlight was fitted with two wires, one of which was permanently attached to the positive diode of the battery, the other having a finger clamp so that it could be moved quickly on and off the negative diode. Tommy busied himself with a file, sharpening the prongs on the pike, using the wire to tie them closer together so that a fish could not fit between the prongs.

I was wearing my NATO Parka, a beanie and wellingtons and Big Joe was wearing his usual farm gear. But then Biddy and Breda decided they too were coming for a bit of *craic* and set about dolling themselves up for the occasion. Biddy put on a pair of stockings and tight little high heels. Breda was doing her lipstick and eyes in the battered mirror nailed to the wall with the transfer of Michael Jackson staring back out at her, retrieved from some skip on a London roadside. The transfer was black so Michael looked white, otherwise he wouldn't have been there.

Big Joe started taking the piss … "where do you think we're going fishing, the fecking Bianconi'. The Bianconi was a restaurant and pub in Killorglin that served fish.

We went outside to test the gear. My task was to operate the battery and light. Big Joe strung the harness over my neck and fitted the battery in at waist level….it weighed a fecking ton…..I then applied the wires to the poles and the car light sent a powerful beam across the yard.

'Turn that fecking thing off' shrieked Biddy hysterically, ' do you want the guards to see us?'

'We're in our own yard on the top of our own mountain you fecking crazy bitch,' Big Joe shot back.

'Ah dad,' clucked Biddy affectionately at her husband.

We all piled into Tommy's two door car. The little brown Dachshund on the fluffy fluorescent yellow shag pile carpet across the back sill nodded accusingly. The shag across the front dash was of an equally objectionable but different hue, with all manner of paraphernalia hanging from the mirror including a leprechaun with a penis larger than his entire body, next to a brass crucifix. There were chrome, mirrors and flashing lights everywhere, and of course a sun roof - a must for all Irish seasons. Biddy, myself and Breda (Clare had retired to Lakeview house with baby Ciaran) stuffed ourselves into the back while big Joe wedged his stiff back into the front passenger seat. Biddy was trying to hide the pike, which was sticking out the back window. Tommy turned the key in the ignition and nothing happened. We remembered that I had the car battery on my lap. Another delay while Tommy replaced the car battery. He returned to the cab and opened the door. The cab light went on. Before he closed the door he also remembered the leprechaun on the mirror, and turned to me with a broad grin:

'Look here, Tim." He pulled the little chain, and the huge penis of the leprechaun leapt to erect. Big Joe ignored this action completely, unable to comprehend youth or the new world. Biddy sighed 'Ah, Tom,' and Breda laughed a deep, dirty laugh. What nobody seemed to notice was that each time the penis shot up, it slapped a very sore looking Jesus in the face.

Finally we took off, with James Last blaring scratchily from the eight track surround-sound speakers.

There were no other cars as we turned off the main road onto the narrow boreen that took us into the lands of Derrynafeana. Here the rivers began on the cusp of Mount Carrountoohil before winding down to Coose Lake, then off the plateau and down through Likkeen Wood, Lough Caragh and onwards to the sea. By day the whole area was a fisherman's paradise.

The night was spectacular. A bright, jewel-like moon had just appeared over the black mountain. The air was crisp and very cold, steam breaking from our mouths as we breathed. The ground crunched, the thick hoar frost providing a slippery surface underfoot. The accompanying sound of water gushing over rocks and reverberating off the stone cliffs, completed the sensational atmosphere.

There was much debate about where we were headed, where we should stop, where we should hide the car and, most of all, what we should do in the event of discovery by the guards. Either I was missing something or the debate was academic. There was one way in and one way out, we either had salmon, batteries, pikes, lights…or we didn't. But none of this stopped Biddy from yelling every few minutes that she could see the guards. The light would go off and we would all dive for cover behind a stone wall for a few minutes before emerging with big Joe telling her once again what a 'fecking crazy bitch' she was.

Finally we were on the river, I got the light on and through the crystal clear water one could see every detail perfectly. There were some fish, but the Boons seemed a little disappointed, so we moved upstream, occasionally slipping into some boggy bit in the dark with Biddy struggling up in her high heels.

When we reached the next level stretch of water, I again fired up the light. Here there were several huge fish, and the whole Boon gang was galvanised. Tommy started stalking along the bank while big Joe positioned himself on a little rise propped up on his stick from where he commanded the operation. Breda stationed herself where the water left the level in a torrent, to cut off the salmons' escape route. Biddy scanned the horizon for the headlights of the guards.

Big Joe issued instructions as if gathering sheep with his dogs in the hills. I was the dog. 'Up a bit, up a bit, up..up..up, now down, down, down move move, down, down....too fecking slow, down , down....uwp, uwp ....move it faster you fucking lazy hoor....'

By then he'd quite forgotten where he was and was simply consumed by the occasion, as were we all. I was charging up and down the bank with the light on this fish then that, trying to follow Tommy's movements, then the pike would be hurled through the water, missed and there'd be a break in proceedings to retrieve the pike, catch our breath and analyze where we'd gone wrong.

It was decided the pool was too big, making it too easy for the salmon to escape. We moved up the river until we found a smaller pool. It was thrashing with fish. Now everyone got involved, Breda standing with her legs astride two rocks above the rushing water and Biddy joining big Joe in shouting instructions.

The fish were shooting up and down, all of us a-shouting and a-screaming, the clandestine nature of the operation entirely forgotten. Breda got so carried away as a fish shot past her that she plunged into the freezing water and tried to catch it with her hands. Everyone ignored her as the pike was hurled into the water and through the body of a massive salmon.

Tommy retrieved the end of the pike and threw it and its heavy load onto the bank. Breda was still thrashing around in the water, big Joe was hollering so loud his voice was echoing back from mount Carrountoohil. Suddenly, Biddy shrieked: 'the guards!!!!!'.

I ripped the clamp from the battery and the scene was thrown into darkness, everyone dived for cover behind a rock or gorse bush and silence prevailed - except for the flap-flap of the expiring salmon on the bank, the pike's prongs embedded in its beautiful body shining silver in the moonlight.

The night's entertainment was at an end. We drove our catch back to the house where it was insisted that I take it – the Boons, it transpired, never ate fish. It was only for sport. So I took the fish home and gutted it, and found it full of roe, which sent me into of spiral of guilt and remorse and promises about never doing it again. Clare and I ate it. It was horrible. I rationalised that it we had got our just dessert, so to speak.

A week later, Tommy arrived on our doorstep with a bag filled with eight huge salmon and announced that ' the boys went out for some sport a few nights after to prove how it's really done' I thanked him and gave the fish a decent burial in the back garden.

Biddy promised to introduce us to her 'best friend' Sheila, who was married to Seamus Sheehan. The alliterative couple had two sibilant children, Sera and Sean.

'They live very close to your home in Dromleagh on the lands of Gortagreenane.' She told us. 'Their daughter Sera might be willing to babysit Ciaran and give you a bit of a break.'

This was a very interesting proposition - especially to Clare, who'd not been parted for a minute from our dear son since we'd arrived in Ireland. The day came and we went down to Sheila's house for tea, heralding the start of a new relationship between our family and the Sheehans. Co-incidentally, it was the Sheehan's turn for 'stations' that year and we were promptly invited. Sheila spent the next few weeks industriously sprucing up the family house for 'stations'. Not a detail was left unattended to. Besides ensuring that the house and garden were immaculate, Sheila personally attended to certain DIY necessities – a leaking toilet was repaired and some new lino laid over the old tatty piece, a window was reputtied and painted.

Father O'Dowd arrived and in time-honored fashion was treated with great reverence. A little party led by Sheila formally welcomed him on the drive, and ushered him into the house. He moved straight to the formalities, conducting the prayers and a little singing, the blessing and a short speech on the meaning and importance of the occasion. Then, just when the guests were beginning to sense an end to their suffering and the onset of tea and cake, the wily cleric announced that he hadn't seen too many of the assembled throng at confession recently. The company froze as he asked Sheila if he could move to one of the bedrooms where he would hear their doubtless urgent confessions.

The stationers were more than put out by this development. While Sheila was setting up the canon in a bedroom, the valley folk begin a lively debate about who should be the first sinner to repent. There were no volunteers - everyone was stunned at having to go at all, let alone be the first. Fortunately, Maire Houlihan had brought her eldest son, Timmy-John, who was eight. She turned on him, much to the relief of the others, and ordered him to get into the bedroom with Father O'Dowd .

Timmy-John looked frankly petrified: 'What should I say?' he pleaded.

'Tell him your sins,' said his mother.

'I haven't got any,'

'Of course you have, you bold little eedjit' she said.

'Like what?'

'Just make something up,' someone suggested helpfully.

'Like what?' he said even more desperately.

'Tell him you lied to your mother,' said his mother.

'But I didn't, mam.'

Mrs Houlihan had had enough of such existential nonsense. 'For God's sake get in there and just tell him you did, you thick fool, and if you don't move fast your father will give you a healthy land when he gets home tonight,' she hissed.

The unhappy boy went in to lie that he lied, followed one by one by those with more time to make up their stories. We did not attend the prayers in the morning, but chose instead to visit the house for drinks in the evening.

We were solemnly ushered into the living room, which was overwhelmed by a thick scarlet carpet with massive roses on it and a gargantuan bowl of plastic flowers on a table. Around the edges were chairs filled with family members. 'This is Seamus' brothers' wife Nora, from the Black Valley, they're still on the family farm doing the sheep, she's related to the Mullane's, you know the ones that sold you the cottage, as a matter of fact they're also distant cousins of mine.' I ended up realising that most people were related, and not all that distantly either.

It was not the most dynamic gathering I'd ever attended, and I was relieved when Biddy and big Joe arrived, knowing that with them it wouldn't be long before some 'craic' was started. It happened even sooner than I thought. Big Joe and Biddy were barely settled into chairs with drinks in hand before the fun began.

' Do you remember everybody?' Sheila asked them.

'No' said big Joe, pointing at Nora, 'and who's this young gal here?'

'That's our cousin Nora from the Black Valley, you know her,' said Sheila, 'She's married to Seamus' brother.'

'Nora?' asked big Joe, astonishment dawning: 'that little Nora from the black valley, with the brother that was drowned in the Blackwater?'

'That's me,' said Nora in a shy, uncomfortable kind of way. Clearly not one of life's big winners, Nora seemed moved that big Joe should remember her at all.

'It can't be,' said big Joe. 'You were the ugliest thing in all these blashted hills, so you were.'

'Ah, Dad,' Biddy admonished her husband, 'What a thing to say.'

The general intake of breath seemed only to goad him on.

'No, don't you remember how fecking ugly she was? How we all used to laugh and joke about how even the rams would be turning a blind eye in her direction?'

Poor Nora - along with Biddy and the rest of the stationers – squirmed. But Big Joe was not one for noticing such social torments. His forte was spotting a stray sheep from a thousand metres, not an injured woman across the room.

'She was the size of a fecking midget, she had shite growing all over her face and she had nothing to hold onto. What do you want me to say? She was a class of a Rose of Tralee? But ... she's gotten a whole lot better now.'

A sigh of relief breezed through the party, and even Nora, though still somewhat stunned, got some of her colour back.

Then big Joe addressed her directly again.

'You've gotten a whole lot better now, gerl' he said, full of admiration.'I didn't even know it was you. How many children have you got?'

'Five.'

'I'm not surprised,' he said.

Nora practically sobbed with gratitude.

8. OUTFOXING THE BANKER

We had already met Ned The Banker Liddy at Paddy O'Sullivan's stations. The Banker was so called because he couldn't bear to part with any money. This was a family trait, his father having being known as The Banker before Ned and his father before that. Unlike anybody else we had the pleasure to come to know in Ireland, Ned's tightfistedness extended even into the domain of alcohol. This was just as well, as he was unable to 'take his drink' as the expression went. His unwillingness to open his wallet in the pub, coupled with his loss of control after taking the alcohol, were an unfortunate combination, because on such occasions when drink was free, Ned inevitably made a fool of himself.

Ned was the youngest of nine children, all of whom had migrated to Boston, leaving him the family's last remaining piece of land. The land was too small and too poor to support more than one person; and even that person had to work hard and benefit from both social security and the European Community sheep quota money, to make a meager living. Ned lived with his niece, Eileen, his oldest sister's daughter. Eileen had been born and raised in Boston and on a visit back from the United States to the ancestral lands, she had become pregnant. She never returned to America.

The valley folk expressed either pious outrage at her pregnancy, or poured on the scorn, depending on the occasion and the company. More accurately, pious outrage was expressed when sober, scorn when drunk. The source of local hostility was only in part a response to Eileen's suspicious pregnancy. Though she was a Liddy family member, returned to her roots (an aspect that the valley folk might have taken as complimentary), she remained a foreigner, a 'blow-in', and she might as well have been from outer space.

It didn't matter what she did to involve herself in the ways, the habits, the work ethic, or the social life of the valley folk, nobody could trust *that* accent. She worked with Ned at the sheep, at the cows, at the turf , in fact at every farming activity lot - as an equal. You would see her ferrying the flock across the road in a howling gale, in yellow rain suit and wellingtons, covered in mud and shit, blonde hair matted across her face, and she would smile happily and wave. But she was just a 'fecking Yank'. After the baby, she was a 'fecking Yank hoor'.

The baby was called little Ned. The men of the valley raised the subject of the baby's origins with 'the banker' only when many pints had been buried in the belly. And the story from 'the banker' was always the same. 'It was a student tourist who was passing through the valley'. This explanation raised howls of derision, which forced Ned to raise his fists to defend the pride of the family Liddy. He would regularly return home with a bruised forehead or crooked swollen nose, but this was part of the pleasure of the evening. Nothing was ever remembered the following day.

Nobody asked Eileen to verify the truth of this story. She was ignored, and that was fine by her. Her acceptance of this ostracization spoke volumes about what she might have to endure were she to return to the community in Boston.

As the years went by, little Ned grew to be the spitting image of The Banker. He loved the farm, and even more so than the other children in the valley, he became a crucial part of the Liddy farming staff. By the time he was ten, he almost never went to school anymore and resembled The Banker in every detail, including his clothes, which were Banker hand me downs.

Around this time a new rumour swept the valley: Eileen was pregnant again. This time there could be no 'student passing through' excuses. Whenever the valley folk were together at stations, at a wake or in church, there would be whisperings:

'Don't you agree she's put on weight all of a sudden?'

'Did you notice she isn't seen outside anymore?'

'There was a pregnant woman seen at Doctor Billie's lasht week...'

And so it went on, until after another couple of months, the tune changed:

'Have you noticed Eileen's gone all thin, and she doesn't wear them coats anymore?''

'Have you noticed any baby's clothes on the clothes line?'

'Of course not, that Yank bitch is too high and mighty to use nappies, she's using them plastic disposables, the lazy hoor'.

Whatever Eileen did or didn't do, was wrong and proof that she'd had another baby.

We contributed vigorously to the debate. When asked if we'd noticed anything peculiar – after all, we were, as the crow flies, the nearest neighbours – we said we hadn't, but promised to keep the binoculars trained on the kitchen window and report any signs of babies.

The months went by, and although Eileen's every move and habit was reported and scrutinised, no baby emerged from the house. When the story could be justified no longer, new bits of fiction were set down.

'Remember when she was away for that week in August? The dirty hoor must have been to America and had an abortion, God help us all!'

Lastly and most outrageously, but at least definitively, there was this rumour: 'She stuffed the poor cratur in a bag and took it to the dump.' Another fairytale ground to an end, but it had kept the valley rocking for months.

There was another member of Ned Liddy's household, an old uncle who'd been called Strong Jim his whole life, which was now drawing to an end at the overripe age of ninety five. He was known to have lived the life of a 'blaguard', always on the wrong side of the law, always in trouble with the guards, no permanent home or family, and at the age of seventy, he'd finally needed to settle down and put up his travel weary feet. Life on the road was not an easy thing. He had no means and could not pay his way. The pension for a single man like him, with no visible past bar a few notes in police diaries around the country, was not sufficient to put a meal a day on the table. But Strong Jim had spent his life busking and he was not about to be defeated by retirement. So he went blind. This meant a disability allowance to supplement the pension, which represented a sum that could buy his way into The Bankers house. The Banker appreciated every bit of help he could get.

Two of the young lads in the valley, Christy Houlihan and Thady Mor, hearing all the talk surrounding Strong Jim's conversion to blindness, decided to undertake an investigation of their own. The plan involved the two of them arriving unannounced at Ned's house when they knew Strong Jim to be there alone. They would find some pretext on which to gain an invitation into the house from their quarry, and when it was time to leave, only Christy would go. Thady would stay in the house and see just how blind strong Jim really was. Clever as it was, not all the permutations of the plan were thought through. If Strong Jim was blind, the lad would witness a blind man moving around the house and that would be that. If Strong Jim wasn't blind... well, the course of action in this event had not been plotted.

Strong Jim was a gregarious fellow. When he heard who was at the door, he was very welcoming and looked forward to passing some time in idle chit-chat with the lads from the valley. In fact he felt a little honoured that such young strapping lads should want to pass some time with an old man like himself. He instructed them to put the kettle on the range and make tea all round, and there was a little flagon of poitín in the bottom of the turf box; he was sure the boys were old enough for a wee taste.

The usual conversation trawled through the weather, the sheep, the fox, the cows, the turf, the hay, the pub. Then Strong Jim entertained the lads with some of the stories from his hugely eventful life on the road, one of which was his escape from Killorglin.

He'd been in an unspecified 'spot of bother' with the guards and in the ensuing search for Jim, all four entry and exit roads to the town had been blocked by a posse. Strong Jim effected his escape by swimming across the Laune river under cover of darkness. The Laune river is some sixty metres across in Killorglin, sixty metres of treacherous water on account of its proximity to the sea and the consequent tidal action. Strong Jim was no different from the rest of the populace in that he couldn't swim. In fact he was not known for ever having been seen to take a bath, let alone a swim. But somehow he managed to forge that river and remain beyond the law's reach once again. Strong Jim's stories piled up and in this way an entertaining afternoon was passed.

When the boys announced that it was time to go, Strong Jim asked them to put away the cups and bottle on account of the difficulty he had with these things in his blind state.

The lads led the way down the passage from the kitchen where they'd been sitting at the range, to the front door with Thady saying noisy good-byes. He opened the front door ahead of the other two but instead of passing through he ducked right, through the door into the living room and stood there, as quietly as possible. Christy closed the front door, shouting farewells to Strong Jim who was feeling his way down the walls of the passage to the front door which, Thady noticed, he carefully locked.

Hearing Strong Jim go back down the passage to the kitchen, Thady tiptoed to the door and stuck his head out into the passage and looked towards the kitchen. He was taken aback to see Strong Jim standing in the kitchen doorway, staring straight back at him. Thady quickly withdrew his head, but then he remembered that Strong Jim was blind, so he couldn't have seen him, could he? A few seconds later, he heard strong Jim shuffling towards him down the passage.

As quickly and quietly as he could, Thady hid behind a chair in the living room. Strong Jim felt his way into the room and over to the radio, fiddling with the knobs until it was on. Finally, he sat down in the chair behind which Thady was standing. Thady had to stand dead still, hoping that neither his breath nor his farm smell would give him away. Wondering if anybody else might be home soon, he thought about how to escape, but Strong Jim was sitting in such a way that he would have to clamber over him to get out from behind the chair. He stood like this for an hour, looking down at the top of Strong Jim's head. Then Strong Jim got up and went back across the room and out the door into the passage. The radio was still on, and Thady could not hear where Strong Jim might be in the bungalow. Still, Thady was exhausted and decided to make his escape through the front door, investigation complete or not. He got to the door of the living room and stepped into the passage. Strong Jim's fist smashed into the side of his head. Thady fell from the blow and the shock. Strong Jim was on him, sitting astride his body, fisting his face left, right, left, right. He might have been seventy but he'd lived a life on the road, and he knew how to give someone a hiding. When Thady was reduced to a groaning, bloody mess, Strong Jim got off him, opened the front door and threw him into the mud and rain. Christy, who'd been hiding outside, cold and wet, got Thady to his feet and dragged him home.

The valley folk did not believe that the result was conclusive either way, but there were no more volunteers for putting Strong Jim to the test.

I met Strong Jim twenty five years after he gave Thady a hiding. He was ninety-five and it was on the day before he died. The whole valley knew that Strong Jim was dying. While Ned Liddy had paid us a few formal visits *a la* Paddy O'Sullivan, we'd never reciprocated. While the neglect of this social responsibility was just about acceptable, our failure to attend the formal functions such as stations, weddings, funerals and wakes, was not.

These visits were not Clare's bag, so the job always fell to me. Before arriving in Ireland, I'd been to a couple of funerals, but I'd never actually seen a body. In Ireland I got close-up to corpses every two months on average – and I still wasn't use to it. Now I was going to see someone who was going to die tomorrow. At least with a corpse, there can be no conversation. What does a person, with no experience in these things, say to someone who can still answer back? I arrived at the door, hoping, no praying (all of a sudden thinking of myself as an agnostic rather than an atheist) that someone else would be visiting the patient too. No luck. Eileen opened the door, and all polite and friendly, showed me straight through to Strong Jim's room, where he lay swaddled in white sheets. Even with no experience in such things I could see the old man was close to breathing his last.

'Jim, Jim!' Eileen shouted in her American accent in his ear, 'this is Tim, from across the valley like, the bloke from Africa we've been telling you about. Come all the way from Africa to the valley, say hello Jim, say hello'

'Hello, Jim' I said, taking his hand that Eileen has put into mine.

'Argh' he replied.

And with that, Eileen left the room. It was just me and Jim. His eyes were sunken, his hair wispy, his skull showed clearly through the drawn skin, matching the whiteness of the sheets. He looked at me, I forgot he was supposed to be blind, had he forgotten he was blind? I was gulping like a fish full of oxygen, just like him.

'You're looking…er…strong,' I said, and instantly couldn't believe I'd said it.

'No,' he croaked, 'I'm weak … I'm … dying'.

There had never been an occasion up to that point in my life when I had thought that saying nothing would be better than saying something. This was a first. I decided to simply sit it out in silence until someone came in there and saved me.

Some minutes went by, then Eileen was back chit-chatting about this and that, and I said 'goodbye Jim' and made my escape. The next day Strong Jim did indeed die, taking the secret of his blindness with him.

During our second spring in the cottage, Ned The Banker decided that his farming techniques needed the assistance of technology. This took the form of the purchase of a 'gas gun', a little device powered by a bottle of compressed gas, which took a predetermined amount of time to reach a certain pressure. The pressure would then release, causing a sound much like that of a shotgun. The object was to scare the fox. The gun would be set up in the field where the ewes were lambing, and bang away all night, keeping the lambs safe but sleepless. Ned's logic was that sheep would be content to live beneath the protective umbrella of ceaseless explosions, while foxes wouldn't come anywhere near it.

Across the valley, we became aware of the clockwork gunshots, in much the same manner as we had become aware of Daniel Casey's earthmoving machine at Lakeview House. It depended on the weather. If there was a howling gale down the valley, we heard nothing. If it was a beautiful, wide-skied night, it was as if we were in the trenches. In short, the noise seldom bothered us thanks to Ireland seldom being blessed with clear skies.

But the fox has eluded man's most sophisticated and determined efforts to cause its extinction. The traps, the guns, the poisoned meats strewn across the countryside, had caused the virtual elimination of some other species, especially birds of prey like the peregrine falcon. And although such efforts regularly caused the death of farmers' own sheep dogs, the fox remained at large. Although it was forced to live a difficult and harassed existence, its hardy species could still be found across the length and breadth of the Irish countryside.

I once happened to be repairing a door at Ger Mullane's farm and was privy to a fox hunting planning session. Four or five burly farmers sporting bad teeth, stubble, and all manner of old blunderbusses (mostly homemade reminders of ancient skirmishes against the English), tucked into a massive black-pudding fry-up and discussed ways of outwitting the fox.

There were more 'fecks', 'fucks' 'cunts' and 'hoors' then there was solid planning from what I could tell, but that was the way with most things. Purely by coincidence, on my way home that day, I had spotted a fox crossing the country lane ahead of my car. It looked physically powerful in that sinewy way, agile, fast, and perfectly balanced by its big bushy red tail. It was an impressive enough sight to convince me that the farmers would not easily extinguish the species. That evening I arrived home to discover our six kittens lying in clinically dismembered bits all over the garden. The fox had to eat.

Ned The Banker's fake gun did have curiosity value for me, as it seemed to assume that fox would be scared of the bang. Given the cunning nature of the fox, and its ability thus far to have lived in defiance of the will of man, I suspected that this new device was more likely to act as a loud hailer than a deterrent, relaying to the fox the exact position of the newly-born lambs. And every year, like clockwork, the night the gun was turned on, the happy fox would tuck into some fresh lamb and Ned The Banker slept sound knowing that his lambs were living under the protective umbrella of his gas banger. It was an arrangement that all parties were happy with, except possibly the lamb who was new enough in the world not to know any difference anyway.

9. THE PATTER OF LITTLE WELLIES

Our daughter Gina was conceived and born in Ireland, but it was the birth of our son Ciaran, four years earlier that had been one of the principal reasons for us leaving London to live in County Kerry. Simply put, we did not want to bring up a child on the streets of London. We lived in a terraced row in Finsbury Park (on the Victoria and Piccadilly line for people who judge their fellow Londoners by tube), bordering Islington (for the estate agents) and round the corner from Arsenal football stadium (for the rest). We foresaw that we would never have the means to propel ourselves sufficiently northwards and outwards (leapfrogging Dagenham, South Norwood and Heathrow) to get our kids into leafier environs. This being the case we decided to leave altogether. County Kerry rolled nicely off the tongue, and it was certainly green.

While living in London it had become a regular habit of ours to eat out on a Friday night. The last Friday of August 1989 was no different, except that Clare was nine months and a week pregnant. We sensibly decided not to stray too far from home, and the Indian restaurant at the corner of our street seemed just the ticket. We took a warm summer's evening stroll. On Blackstock Road, near the Gunners Arms and across the way from the Kopfe-Kebab take-away, we walked into an otherwise empty restaurant named Beauty, a bizarre name even by Blackstock Road's exotic standards. The decor, the ambiance, the menu and the personnel were like any one of a thousand local Indian restaurants in London. It was only the name which, on any other evening would have sent us running for the cover of something more familiar like a Taj Mahal or New Delhi or even the Anglo-Asian Tandoori if we happened to be in an ironic pro-empire mood. But this was not any other evening, and in we went.

Clare usually kept away from anything too rich, opting for a chicken korma, or a biryani. But on this particular evening, in her most delicate state, Clare's menu-finger alighted on the prawn bhuna and nothing could budge it. The prawn bhuna came, and went into Clare's stomach where it was separated from our soon to emerge son by the skin of an intestine and little else. Through the translucent skin he must have seen it coming and sensibly decided he'd be better off out of there. Before the meal was over, Clare began to wince and both of us sat trying to ward off panic. We reminded each other that labour can be a long process, and that it was highly unlikely that the baby would be landing on the floor of Beauty. We tried to recall the pre-natal lessons and after a bit of disciplined breathing, with me doing the counting, a semblance of control was re-established. I went to the back of the restaurant to find the proprietor. He looked nervous and slightly put out that I wanted to pay the bill so fast. We walked the two hundred yards back home, Clare experiencing several sharp pangs along the way.

It was just 8pm. At home we began to calm down. Remembering the advice from the pre-natal classes, we went about methodically putting the hospital bag together and making what other preparations were necessary. Clare's labour pains had subsided, and there seemed no real urgency to head for the hospital. Clare was, under the circumstances, comfortable, and we were confident that everything – including us - was under control. We turned on the TV, and there, with appropriate absurdity, was a capering Kenneth Williams in Carry-On Nurse. The prawn bhuna was forgotten, at least by myself, as was the impending event.

At midnight I was jolted out of 'Carry On' mode by Clare, whose labour pains had reached a level of intensity and regularity to warrant making the ten minute drive to Whittington Hospital at the top of Holloway road. We were ushered into a room and introduced to the midwife, who efficiently began her ministrations. Various nurses and doctors popped in, inspecting equipment and monitoring progress, and all was made ready for the big push.

Clare's waters broke on schedule and all appeared to be progressing according to plan – except that Clare didn't seem to be putting maximum effort into the pushing, no matter how much urging she received from the midwife and myself. Only afterwards did she confide her fear the pressure of pushing might, instead of delivering our son into the world, dislodge the curried prawns from their dark cavern and send them unceremoniously back into the world not one inch from where our darling son was scheduled to emerge.

Clare knew with dreadful clarity that ordering the prawns had been throwing caution to the winds, so to speak, but there was precious little she could do about it now – except not push. The fear became so intense that she called for an epidural, the logic being that this would anaesthetize the prawns long enough for her to concentrate all her energies on the real task at hand. It didn't work, but fortunately by the time the anesthetic started wearing off, there appeared to be some progress and finally, just when foetal stress seemed to be setting in, our son popped out, short on breath and needing to be immediately oxygenated. Somehow this hardly seemed surprising.

In the couple of days that followed, Clare's fitness as a breast-feeding mother was monitored, and Ciaran was thoroughly checked for imperfections.

We were pleasantly surprised to learn that all that was 'missing' was a testicle - not that he didn't have it, rather that it was tucked up out of sight in his groin. The doctor casually mentioned that if it didn't come down of its own accord within three years, a small procedure might be required to get it swinging in the right location. We were assured by the smooth talking medical personnel that this was 'not entirely unusual'- whatever that favourite double negative of the medical fraternity is supposed to mean.

Some days later we received the following note from the midwife:

Dear Clare and Tim,

I felt I would like to share a few thoughts with you both, concerning the recent arrival of your beautiful son, safely into the world.

It was such a pleasure, not to mention a privilege, to be able to share in such a precious time in both your lives. Working with you in the small hours of the night, and sharing an exciting dawn that would spread light upon a day that you will never forget, will be amongst my fondest memories of a midwife in England.

Please send me some copies of the photographs you took Tim, soon after delivery. These will be placed in my auto biography depicting for me, the ultimate midwifery experience. Thank you for allowing me to share this with you.

Much love,

Brenda Burton (the midwife).

That a hardened pro with countless deliveries under her belt could still find joy in each delivery, touched our hearts. Though I couldn't help wondering how the sentiment might have differed if Brenda had known that Clare was as concerned about the whereabouts of a prawn bhuna as she was about her baby.

The arrival of our daughter four years later was an altogether different affair. Firstly, we were by then living in the backwoods of Ireland, a two and a half hour car journey from the City of Cork and with only an unreliable old Irish banger to get us there. In addition, Erinville Hospital offered epidurals only on Tuesdays and Thursdays thanks to budget restraints and the limited availability of trained staff.

It was, remarkably, a Friday night again when the same set of events began to unfold. Fortunately this time we were at home - probably due to the absence of restaurants in the Irish backwoods, particularly Indian ones. At this point in our lives it was doubtful we'd have had the money to splurge on restaurants anyhow. We were simultaneously struck by the same panicky thought: Friday – no epidurals.

We had a cup of tea (the closest prawn being five miles away snuggled up in its ocean bed) with Philippa, Clare's sister who had arrived from Rome to look after Ciaran while we handled the birth. Remembering our first experience, even drinking the tea had us contemplating what ramifications there might be.

We arrived in Cork incident free, and were even relaxed enough to have a drive around the city before heading to the hospital at 3am. At reception there was a bit of a commotion. There was a young, very distressed woman, a glitzy dress stretched over her pregnant bump, her face running with mascara. There was talk of 'the tinker woman' having been kicked 'by her boyfriend' in her stomach. We checked in, and were shown to a room with two beds in it and once again the wait began. This time the wait was curtailed by the immediate onset of big, regular contractions. I pushed Clare squirming in a wheel-chair, into the delivery ward in which there were also two beds. The other bed was already occupied, and a plastic curtain was hastily drawn across it.

Once again I manned the top end while the midwife went below. At this point I volunteered that it was probably my turn to go below, but the midwife said her employment contract insisted that she woman that location. She didn't laugh either.

This time round Clare was an altogether different animal. She heaved and puffed, and pushed and shoved like a creature possessed, with me whispering intermittent encouragement in her ear...no epidural, no epidural. What motivated her further, and it's a horrible thing to say, was that the woman the other side of the thin plastic curtain was having a bad time of it. She seemed to be getting nowhere, judging by the sobbing and screams of pain and frustration that rent the room. No husband or relative was present. In Ireland having babies was woman's work.

Clare has often reminded me that during this birth, I hurriedly left the room for a while, saying that I couldn't breathe and was about to faint, but I don't remember.

It wasn't long before I heard a noise like a Christmas turkey being released from a plastic bag, and there was our baby daughter with a weirdly shaped head, covered in various flotsam and jetsam, but beautiful all the same. She was wrapped in a blanket, and we were hastily shown the door to another lonely room with a tiny window that looked out over the bleak, grey, unmoving Cork city at 6:30 on a drizzly Saturday morning.

Clare looked clapped. The effort she put into this one had knocked her out completely. In fact she had damaged her back, and remains injured to this day from that final determined push.

We returned to the two-bed ward with the TV in the middle, and Clare settled into bed with Gina draped across her. She needed rest. I hung around for an hour or so, blinked into a fresh early morning shower of rain, and drove home, bearing the good news.

The rest of that day and night was spent back at the cottage at Droumleagh. The following morning I arrived back at the hospital with an excited Ciaran and Philippa in tow, to see that the first bed was now occupied by the young – still pregnant - woman we had seen at reception on our arrival. The TV was on, with the volume turned down. Clare looked exhausted and absolutely distraught.

It transpired that the runny mascara woman had arrived to fill the second bed in Clare's ward shortly after I had left the day before, and had settled down nice and cosy with a fag and a little flagon of whisky which she kept hidden under the bedclothes. The day had passed off fairly peacefully but by nightfall the TV was turned up at full volume. The traveler woman had described to Clare the beating she had suffered at the hands of 'her boyfriend'.

'And if he finds me here, I'm dead meat,' she announced, sending shivers down Claire's spine imagining the kind of event she might have to endure in that little ward.

The hospital had checked the woman in for observation, but a nurse confided later that she was a regular who arrived every few months injured and broken and in desperate need of a bath and a few days respite from her daily struggle. The nurses had taken pity on the woman and allowed her to use to place like a shelter every now and then or else 'the poor cratur would be dead, for sure.'

With the TV at full blast, Clare hit the panic button but no one came. She needed rest and she wasn't going to get it under these circumstances, but she didn't have the energy to confront the woman about the blaring TV, the booze or the fags. So, as the baby was sleeping, Clare got up and sat outside the ward. As it was 2:30 a.m. on a Sunday morning there wasn't much activity in the passage and it was some time before a nurse happened along to find Clare in floods of tears. Her room mate was then so full of remorse that it was positively energy sapping. She couldn't do enough to make amends, although the TV stayed on albeit with the sound turned down.

The following evening the face of a man did indeed appear around the corner. The woman had dressed and made up as if his arrival was expected, and she was gone, much to Clare's relief and the nurses' annoyance. The bed was made up fresh, and it wasn't long before a new mum and offspring took occupation. The curtain was pulled tight around the new arrivals, hiding the shock and pain of the new baby's cleft palate and hare-lip, leaving a family to grieve and plan as best they could for a life quite different to that which they'd been dreaming of a few hours earlier. Our celebrations took on a new dimension - quiet appreciation of the lucky cards we'd been dealt.

The rest was fairly predictable. Ciaran, then three, was confused, jealous and very brave. We have a picture of him and the baby which says it all. His arm is around Gina, no doubt because we told him to put it there, and there is the most pathetic smile on his face. We had obviously told him to smile, possibly the first of many false smiles of his life.

The birth of every child is accompanied by the selection of a name saga. We got off lightly in Ciaran's case. He was born in London after we'd decided to move to Ireland, so we thought it would make sense to give him an Irish name. We only knew two – Ciaran and Liam, and we kept on forgetting to buy an Irish names book until it was too late. Someone said that Liam was Irish for William. A royal English William had just been born, so Ciaran it was. The process turned out to be a happy exception to the saga rule.

Not so the second child, a girl born in Ireland. Clare and I had written down a list of some thirty possible names and were constantly trying to cut it down without success. Then one day while searching for a telephone number in one of Clare's more private diaries I came upon a secret list, headed by the beautiful but foreign 'Juanita'. Without a moment's hesitation I confronted Clare.

'So Juanita heads your list of possible names for the baby,' I accused her. There followed a massive row about what I was doing reading through her private journals, before we could get onto a row about the name.

'Well I think it's a great name,' asserted Clare jutting her chin into the air.

'Yeah, so do I,' I said, 'but it's Mexican.'

'What have you got against the Mexicans now?'

'This is not Mexico.'

'So are you suggesting we ought to have an Irish name then?' said Clare, cocking her gun triggers in readiness to shoot me down.

'Yes,' I said, 'it makes sense ... and I quite like Irish girls names.'

'Mention some of the ones you like,' said Clare knowingly.

'Well, there's ...ah... Siobhan or Aoife, or what about Finnualla..... Grainne..... or Aoibheann.'

'Those aren't names,' laughed Clare, 'those are groups of letters that fell out of a Scrabble box.

'So what are we left with then? An Australian Sheila, an Irish Colleen or a Catholic Mary?.'

Clare raised the white flag. 'At the end of the day it doesn't make much difference. After all, we haven't called Ciaran by his name since the day he was born. So she'll probably be called Fifi-trixabell or Tigerlily or Heavenlyhirana until she's old enough to be called plain old Smart-Arse like the rest of us.'

'Quite right,' I said, happy that we had found some common, if cynical, ground. 'Let's just write some film star names on the dart board and throw a dart.'

And so our darling daughter was named Gina.

Ciaran had another good reason to smile falsely. The three years was up and his testicle had not descended.

At Tralee General Hospital we met the general surgeon, a big, unshaven man who made his smart white coat look shabby. After a cursory glance at Ciaran and without having deigned to address me at all, he told his assistant nurse to book the theatre. The consultation was over in under a minute, and I was left holding Ciaran in the passage, wondering whether I'd done enough to protect my child's best interests. To compensate I asked the harassed receptionist if this was a big operation.

'No' she said, 'but you know they don't just cut without a general anaesthetic.' I wished I hadn't asked her at all. This seemed to be a place where the less said, the better.

I did notice a poster on the wall drawing attention to "Your rights". I paid it no mind.

The operation was to take place on Friday at 14:30hrs, we were to be there suitably ahead of schedule. Clare and I read the baby manuals which suggested preparing the child by explaining what would be happening in a truthful, but non-threatening kind of way. Our first attempt at reassurance resulted in his horrified query:

'Are they going to cut my winky off?'

'No, no, *no,* they aren't going anywhere near your winky,' I said and showed him where I wildly guessed there might be a little cut in his groin. That nobody would cut his winky off was about the only thing I felt sure of.

We arrived at the hospital and I cast around for the surgeon with a view to asking a few last-minute questions, but no such luck. He was in theatre, involved in a never-ending string of life saving procedures, no doubt. I waved pitiably to Ciaran, so small on the trolley, but he looked at me with total confidence and without fear. Clearly, the winky preservation speech had worked.

I sat outside the theatre feeling pretty OK myself: after all, this was a very simple procedure. What could possibly go wrong? The worst-case scenario that my untrained mind could think of was that the testicle would be squashed and might not work properly. In a world of multiple sclerosis, leukemia, bone cancer, blindness, autism and AIDS, I told myself that this was small potatoes.

After a much longer wait than I had anticipated, sufficient for me to start thinking of other things that could go wrong in the theatre, like a shot of contaminated penicillin or a slipping scalpel that severed the Iliac artery, Ciaran was wheeled out looking even smaller than when he was wheeled in, now silent, unmoving under the bedclothes. Once again I was treated with disdain, this time by the nursing aids whose expressions indicated that I was getting in the way of their important work.

He was deposited in the children's ward and I took up position next to his bed. Soon his eyes flicked open, followed by that uncomfortable jolt to consciousness that often accompanies an awakening from anesthetic. He saw me and settled back again with eyes shut, contemplating where he was and what was happening. He then pulled himself into sitting position, and in doing so realized that under the bedclothes skulked a changed and therefore unknown part of his anatomy. He started pulling the blanket off and I rose to assist, folding the white blanket back to reveal his hospital gown with two little white stick legs protruding from it. Ciaran pulled up his gown to expose a ghastly sight. In the position of his appendix there was a two inch stitched gash with yellow antiseptic highlighting the wound, but much worse, the end of his penis was bound with some bloody gauze. He'd been circumcised.

'They did cut off my winky, Dad,' he said almost resigned, but his look at me said so much more. It was one of inevitability, he knew it was going to happen no matter what I said, and because of that he still trusted me.

I was beyond shock. I couldn't understand it, there appeared to be no action in the vicinity of his testes, and he'd been circumcised. I went in search of a nurse.

'Where is the doctor?' I demanded angrily.

'Oh no,' said the nurse, 'you wouldn't be seeing the doctor now. Besides it's the weekend.' - the implication being that even if it wasn't the weekend, doctors are God, you don't call them, they call you.

'But my boy has been circumcised.' I protested.

'Well, what did you expect then?"

"The doctor was supposed to just push his testicle down from the groin."

"Now just think of it as getting two for the price of one, and a very nice little bonus at that.' She said with a wink.

'But he didn't need a circumcision, and nobody told us,' I blurted out hopelessly.

'Do you think the surgeon's got time standing round chit-chatting about this and that. If that child got a circumcision, he needed one. Now if you'll excuse me I've work to do.'

The result of my hopeless intervention was that for the entire weekend all the nurses avoided Ciaran's bed with the unappreciative blow-in father like the plague. And the plague was growing under the bedclothes: without any attention to the wound, the circumcision was going septic. On Sunday afternoon they announced that he was being discharged, they needed the bed, and here were some antibiotics which would clear up the infection.

I was happy to get out of there even though I was concerned for his infected winky. For three days and nights I attended to his puss-soaked penis. Every time he passed urine he would scream in agony. I made sure that the antibiotics were religiously consumed. A pathetic image remains with me of Ciaran in that hospital, running down the passage to the kids games and TV room in his tiny white nightshirt, his legs spread wide so that his penis did not touch anything.

A week later he was to return to the hospital for a check-up and to have the stitches removed. We arrived early for the consultation, and this time I read the 'Your rights' poster in the reception area diligently. It described in detail the rights of a patient or guardian to a comprehensive explanation of any medical condition suffered, of any procedure advised, of any medication recommended, basically of anything that might be prescribed within the perimeter fences of that premises. Furthermore it described the efforts that must be made by medical staff to obtain permission where applicable for any procedures to minors, even where the patient might be on the operating table. It seemed to me that the surgeon had breached most of what was written on that poster.

We were marched into his consulting rooms where the nurse ordered Ciaran to remove his pants. Once again the doctor got up and inspected Ciaran without looking at or addressing me at all. He was satisfied and waved at the nurse to get rid of us. I remained stuck to my seat.

'Why'd you give him a circumcision?' I blurted.

'What?' he said, looking up over his glasses at me flushing red with surprise and anger.

'Why'd you circumcise my boy?'

'Because it was necessary.' He was livid and was clearly trying to restrain himself, probably remembering that poster outside.

'When did you decide when it was necessary?'

'When I inspected his penis.' He said deliberately ambiguously.

'Why didn't you inform me?'

'How could I inform you when he's on the operating table?'

'I was outside the door.'

'Forgive me,' he said sarcastically. 'that's most unusual to be waiting outside the operating theatre, I've never heard of it before.'

'Well you've heard of it now. And what's that other cut for, it's nowhere near his testicles, in fact I still don't see his other testicle.'

'Whatever you see and don't see was medically necessary, and I will be happy to defend those decisions to the hospital authorities or medical council.' He was definitely now remembering the poster.

'And you had no written or verbal consent which you require in terms of the rules described by the poster outside your door.' I picked up Ciaran and stomped out of there. I wanted to leave him with the impression that we would be taking the matter further if only to do the next patient a favour. In truth, we had no intention of taking the matter further, because an action against the doctor and state medical services would have been big news in the locality and would have negative social consequences for us living in our valley.

A year later, in another country, we took Ciaran to a general surgeon, who had no explanation for the cut in the region of his appendix, but would not be critical as even internationally the fraternity must stand together. Once again Ciaran went under the knife, and in a two-minute procedure, his testicle was brought down to the correct position. My opinion remains that the original surgeon not only circumcised our son, but performed an appendectomy as well. Two for the price of one.

10. NOT ONLY IN RUSSIA, MR. GOGOL

Sandwiched between Ned Liddy and the O'Sullivans were Jimmy and Joan Foley and their son Liam. Theirs was a particularly useless piece of land in an area whose topography had already been euphemistically classified as 'disadvantaged'. The land, being on the slopes of the Macgillycuddy reeks was steep and very rocky. Where earth covered the rocks, the soil was too thin to yield much grazing. It was almost impossible to get a tractor up those lands, which meant everything had to be done by hand. Any farming done by hand would have to be very hard work for very little reward.

This had not always been so. In days gone by, small patches of land were cleared of loose rock, which was then used to build walls and houses. The nature and extent of this traditional wall building is something to be marveled at. It is a testament to both the energy and desperation of the builders. Motivation must have been quite simple, for without a field there could be no grazing or growing, and without these two there was no food. All the people in the valley remembered their own childhood's, when on weekends, holidays and even on some school days, they were press ganged into clearing tiny patches of land.

Jimmy Foley must have spent almost all of his life's quota of energy clearing the fields in his youth, because the only energy he had left now was enough to raise a jar to his mouth. At the top of one of his very steep and sloping fields was an old Ford Escort. It was clearly visible from our side of the valley. How it got up that hill, was as mysterious as the building of the walls themselves. And this is where Jimmy Foley spent most of his life.

He was forced to get up in the early morning when his wife made ready for work in the town, and his son for school. He'd shave with his hand razor with the single 'Gillette' blade in the misty mirror, mindful to cover the bleeding bits with toilet paper. Jimmy undertook this ritual as a statement of differentiation from the unshaven local farmers. He was skilled, he had a trade, he'd worked on the buildings, he was better than sheep shit and hay.

Then Jimmy would slip on his wellingtons and his worn-out light grey pinstripe suit with the jacket that was too small and tight even over his thin body, and make his way up the hill out of ear and eyeshot of the house, and clamber into the Escort with the comfy old straw and the big coat which he left in there for the warmth. He'd snore away in there all day, and depending on what *craic* he'd had the night before in the pub, he might have to make his way back down in the dark. On occasion when he did oversleep into the night, he would arrive back at the house and describe the tough day he'd had 'at the sheep on the mountain'. He knew he was in no danger of being discovered in the Escort. His wife was contemptuous of farmers, farms, sheep and mostly of Jimmy himself, so she was not likely to be found wandering over the fields in search of a lost, a late or even a *clifted* Jimmy. Liam was similarly uninterested in his father and the farm. The reason Jimmy took off to go and spend the day in the Escort instead of waiting for the family to leave and then sneaking back into bed, was a face-saver for both father and son. Liam was prone to bunking school himself, and there had been several unfortunate meetings in the house between the two idlers. Liam was surprised to hear that there was an Escort up there on the top field. He'd never in his life taken a walk on the farm.

Because his small and sickly looking flock were left to their own devices, of course they strayed wherever they might find a fresh shoot of grass. Consequently Jimmy Foley was always in dispute with Ned The Banker Liddy, his neighbour on the one side, and Paddy and Paudy O'Sullivan on the other because the fresh shoot of grass usually belonged to them. The O'Sullivans usually ignored him - knowing him to be a good-for-nothing, they would get on and repair the fences and walls themselves, and despise him all the more. On the other side, Jimmy and The Banker had something in common. Like The Banker he couldn't take his drink, but, oh, how he loved it. The result was that the two of them would go off for a pint together the best of chums. After a few jars were sunk, Ned's resentment of Jimmy Foley's farming techniques would surface, and the two drunkards would slug it out. One week, Ned would sport a cut eye, the next Jimmy would have a bulbous blue lip. Like the ancient stone walls themselves, that was how it was. Habits around here were cast in stone. Reading Nikolai Gogol's *Dead Souls* at the time, I was struck by how his descriptions of Russian peasants a century earlier described our friends Ned and Jimmy, especially in the passage:

'And what was most strange, and what can only happen in Russia, within a short time he would again meet the friends who had given him such a thorough beating and meet them as though nothing had happened: he, as they say didn't seem to mind and they didn't seem to mind either.'

Not only in Russia, Mr.Gogol.

Besides this regular bit of *craic* that Ned and Jimmy provided for the locals, there were other events in which they would feature prominently to keep the locals laughing. One such event was the wake of Dinny O'Shea.

Dinny O'Shea had been a bachelor, with no family to speak of. He was a quiet-living, dependable soul who never caused anyone any harm. He had put his shoulder to the wheel his whole life, running his farm single-handed, but mucking in with the neighbors to assist with the hay, the silage and the turf, and enjoying a few pints with the lads every now and then. His neighbor, Paul Coffey, was a much younger version of himself, also a bachelor, minding his own business and getting on with his own small farm. The two of them were very close, and when Dinny's time was nearly up, Paul looked after him, seeing to his every need in his last days. Dinny left all his worldly possessions to Paul, the house, the land, the lot. He did make one request of Paul on his deathbed. No expense was to be spared at his wake: the pints must flow until the orders run dry. While Dinny was realistic enough to know that his life was not memorable, he must have taken great pleasure in giving the dice one last throw in death.

In many places in the world not much attention would be paid to such a request. In rural Ireland, a gesture that placed no restriction on the consumption of alcohol was enormously brave. Perhaps this is an opportune moment to take a superficial look at alcohol and its consumption in Ireland, for a thorough investigation would be a tome.

First and foremost, there is the Guinness. Guinness has become an international institution, built on the back of the humble pint of Irish porter. As an alcoholic beverage it cannot have an equal anywhere else in the world. And I say that as a departed blow-in.

There are numerous criteria determining the taste of the pint. They include the volume and speed of the first pull, the angle of the glass, the length of time after the first pull to settle, then repeat for the second pull, to scrape or not to scrape off head, the temperature of the barrel, the temperature of the pub, the nature of the barman, the length of pipe from barrel to tap, how often the pipe is cleaned, the type of water used in the manufacture, the distance of travel from plant to pub, and maybe even the weather.

Guinness aficionados, and that includes anyone who drinks Guinness, are every bit as sophisticated in their analyses and demanding in their requirements, as a wine boffin. As every pub necessarily delivers a different pint, so each individual swears loyal oaths to their pub.

Then there are those who like to move away from the herd, to be special, a mite more circumspect in their drinking habits perhaps. These people actually turn up their noses at Guinness and call for a Murphy's (a Guinness competitor) or a pint of Teaksons. In England they would be called middle class wankers; in Ireland they are ignored, being simply beneath pity.

Thirdly, there are the whisky drinkers, the Bushmills and the Jamesons and John Power. These are the desperadoes who can't wait for the Guinness to settle; they need the whiskey and they need it now, double, double on the rocks.

Lastly, there are the poitin drinkers. This is the local, highly illegal homebrew, a jar or two of which is likely hidden away in every little cottage and bungalow across the land. Poitin is for that special occasion, perhaps late at night when the pub has closed, there's not a drop in the house but the party must go on. It may be in the middle of the day when a friend has arrived and the bottle has remained unopened too long. Poitin's beauty lies in its unpredictability. After a couple of swigs, you may go temporarily blind. You may be charged with unbelievable strength and energy, and start bleating like a ram. The stars could come out in an Irish sky. You could die. Anything can happen, that's the point.

A good night out for a farmer in our valley entailed the consumption of between eighteen and twenty five pints. This was why I didn't go to the pub anymore. I once managed seven pints, by which time there were three more queued up on the counter. The other lads were just warming up, just entering the heat of the night in the pub, loosening their collars and their inhibitions. And already I am in the bog, peeing all over my hand and wondering whether I can make it to the door without falling down and attracting local mockery for ever more.

Unlike the churches in Ireland, the pubs are supposed to shut up shop at certain times. Five minutes before the dreaded hour the pub is sweltering with the sweat of the patrons doing their utmost to down their accumulated pints. The publican is bellowing above the throng, urging them on like the Oxford or Cambridge rowing teams to the finish line. At the dreaded moment he stops shouting, holds his fingers to his lips and explodes in a violent 'ssshhhh ', all manner of foam flying from his vibrating lips in the effort. He is accompanied in this by an ever-increasing number of patrons themselves. When silence reigns in the pub, the publican pulls the curtains over the windows fronting the pub and disappears out the door where he furtively looks up and down the road outside. Satisfied, he returns, closing and bolting the door behind him and flicking the 'off' switch to the light outside with a theatrical flourish. He turns to the patrons, smiling, his arms raised, palms facing the ceiling. A loud cheer goes up, everybody raises their glasses in celebration and dives raucously for a place at the counter to begin the second half of the evening.

The valley folk knew that Dinny O'Shea's wake was going to be a big one. As Dinny's death was not a surprise, there had been time to organise the formalities. He'd been transported down to the town for the embalming, a decent coffin had been procured and all that remained was to prepare the cottage and buy in the necessaries for the wake. It was decided to put Dinny in the coffin for the wake and not leave him on top off the sheets on his cot, purely as a space saving consideration for his was a very small cottage. He'd been dressed in his favorite suit and looked immaculate as he lay nice and comfy, in his dark wooden box.

The cottage consisted of two rooms. There was a lean-to out the back which had served for Dinny's ablutions, but that wouldn't count for tonight's do. The great outdoors would suffice as a receptacle for the processed alcohol. Dinny in his coffin was laid out on the table in the middle of the bedroom, with a few other sticks of furniture and chairs making the small room seem smaller. The single lightbulb was left on, swinging directly over Dinny's corpse.

The refreshments were hardcore, the only nod at food being a few bags of crisps scattered on the living room table and a plate of ham sandwiches donated by a neighbour. The night's conviviality was contained in the crates and crates of booze stacked around the walls. Everything else had been moved out of the room except for the traditional Irish *settle*.

Unsurprisingly, Jimmy Foley and Ned Liddy were the first to arrive. Ned had made a special effort for the occasion, notching up at least as many razor nicks on his face as Jimmy Foley, though Ned's were festooned with pink toilet paper. Ned's excitement at the drink-till-you-drop party plan showed in the rest of his grooming too. He had plastered back his long, matted hair with Brylcreem and he looked like a washed-up beatnik with measles. When the rest of the boyos arrived and noted Ned's decorations, Dinny was forgotten and the *craic* was on. Ned didn't really understand their laughter, but he joined in all the same.

Jimmy Foley took up position on the seat and began ferreting about in the corner with the bottles but Paul came over, warned him off and threw a blanket over the pile. The priest had arrived to say a few words. The men shuffled unwillingly but obediently through to Dinny to hear what a fine and blessed fellow their absent host had been. The priest knew that if he was to drag it out, he'd have even more work to do on the stragglers in his flock, and on a personal level, he wanted to show that he was man of the world enough to know what tonight was really all about. A few Hail Mary's and a can of coke later, and the priest had departed breathing a sigh of relief. He was always nervous when there were no woman about.

Tonight, there were very few, because Dinny had never had much to do with women. And so Dinny's wake felt more and more like a bachelor's party than the end of a life.

The boyos took up residence in the living room close to the crates, leaving Dinny to amuse himself in his bedroom. The room was filling up. Patty Sheahan was there, the whole Boon gang - Big Joe, Little Joe, Conal, Tommy, Eoin, Breda - Donal and Dinny Houlihan, Thady and Muiris Mor, Jimmy Breen, Mikey Coffey. Even Finbar Feneran had torn himself away from the pub to pay his last respects. Little Joe Boon was telling a story about the day he'd been driving back to his farm, behind another car he didn't recognise. The strange car had taken off down the narrow lane fronting Joe's house, at the side of which were sitting his two sheep dogs. Joe watched in disbelief as the car deliberately swerved to run over the two dogs. Little Joe stopped, but the dogs were dead, so he took off after the vehicle which stopped some miles away on another farm. He hopped out of the car and confronted the man.

'Killed a couple strays in the road,' said the culprit, getting out of his car.

"Those weren't strays, those were my sheep dogs,' Joe said.

'Not my problem,' said the man. 'But it sounds like it's yours'. And with that the stranger opened the boot and lifted out a shotgun lying on a blanket. Little Joe wisely decided not to make anything of it, though he did make a mental note of the place and the man's face: this was business to be finished at a later date when the playing field would be more even.

The boyos looked deeply into their glasses. They all remembered those dogs.

'That pup was from the same litter as my dog,' said Jimmy Breen.

'Was that the pup from the same litter as that bitch who works in the bank?' shouted Patty Sheahan, and the assembled gang roared and filled up their glasses.

The stories went round and round, the volume got louder and louder, the glasses were clinking, the howls of laughter were a warm oasis in the drizzly black night. Darkness had already fallen for Jimmy Foley. In customary style he had already passed out on the *settle* in the corner, and the men were having difficulty reaching the crates, even after he fell off the seat and lay prone on the floor. Muiris Mor got a cheer when he put one of Jimmy Foley's feet under each arm and dragged him through to join Dinny O'Shea in the next room.

The black night outside was punctured by the headlights of a car winding its way down the gravel lane to Dinny's cottage. The lights were clearly visible through the tiny window of the living room, and Paul thought he'd better go and check on the newcomer's identity: the arrival of a relative might require a sudden gear shift in the wake's trajectory.

Sure enough, it was an old aunt of Dinny's, somebody who hadn't been seen in these parts for years, but who had a reputation for being extremely capable for a woman of her advanced years.

Paul shot back inside, warned the boyos to calm down, and promised to try to get rid of her as fast as possible. The lads put together another plan while Paul helped the old lady out of her car. She entered the house and was greeted by a throng of desperately sad looking locals. The whole house had a melancholy quietness to it, punctuated only by one of the boyos hiding behind his hand and appearing to sneeze. Paul introduced the old lady to everyone there, one by one, according to the custom.

'Remember Muiris Mor, from Gortnagreenane?'

'I do, I do, and how's young Finnuala, Muiris?'

'Just fine, a bonny girl now, I'd say, thank you.'

'I bet she is. '

Finally, she asked: 'Now where's young Dinny, may the good God bless his soul.' And Paul ushered her through to the bedroom, where the light has been turned off and a single candle lit.

The coffin lid had been closed and the boys had laid Jimmy Foley on top, crossed his arms and neatened him up. The aunt gave a little gasp, and went up close saying a silent prayer, fingers clutching the cross around her neck. The boys crowded into the room behind her, not wanting to miss a single second of the action.

'If I didn't know it was him, I wouldn't have recognised the poor boy,' exclaimed the aunt turning to Paul.

The boys all started coughing at once.

'He doesn't look well, God bless the poor *cratur*' she said, putting two fingers to his cheek.

'He's dead, ma'am' said Paul.

Jimmy Foley breathed faintly.

'Oh look,' she said, ' there's a little bit of air in him'.

Paul pressed his hands together and agreed, 'A little bit of air left in him yet, ma'am.'

Fortunately someone was retching violently and audibly outside the front door.

'Don't trouble yourself any further,' Paul said to the old aunt, who allowed herself to be guided through to the living room and presented with a coke. Someone had managed to retrieve a couple of serviceable ham sandwiches from the floor for presentation to the special visitor. The old aunt departed, the merriment in the small cottage reached fever pitch shortly thereafter and by three in the morning half the party had joined Jimmy Foley passed out wherever they happened to be positioned as the last swigs went down. Others attempted the ride home. Muiris Mor never made it; he was found passed out in his car, which, after traveling some way in the opposite direction from home, he'd crashed into a *ditch*. The hard men, Finbar Feneran, Ned Liddy and Jimmy Foley, returned home two days later, only when every drop of booze had been consumed according to Dinny O'Shea's last wishes and objective: to turn his wake into the stuff of local legend.

A few weeks later we bumped into Paul Coffey again. It was three in the afternoon of a murky grey day and we were at home. We felt the vibration of a car making its way up to our cottage. We didn't recognise the gleaming, well-kept vehicle as it pulled up. Out jumped Paul, and another fellow togged up in town type suit and tie. Stuck to the car's boot was a poster with an ugly mug shot of the man who was now standing before us. It was election time.

'Hello!' called Paul in a long-lost chums voice. 'You know I've always been interested in the politics like, and our man here representing us in the council would like to be finding out how he can be of service to you.'

'Yes,' said the man who was pictured on the poster. 'You know it was us responsible for the new hospital in Tralee, and the new road to Capanalea. So, of course, if there's anything you need …?'

'What's the difference between you and the other party?' I asked.

'Well now, that's an easy one. You see we do things, like, we get things done. The others will promise you the earth and give you nothing.'

'I'm sure they'll probably say the same about you, 'I said, memories of my membership of the looniest of the British loony left stoking me into debating mode.

I had made a stand against the evil South African apartheid regime by fleeing the call to war in Angola. I had been arrested twice in London, once for sticking up a poster, and , well the other, that's a story for another time. I had marched in countless demonstrations against the Prevention of Terrorism Act, in support of Bobby sands, against racism, the National front, the British movement. I had sold rags of the Revolutionary Communist tendency in Brick Lane, in East Ham and in every god forsaken housing estate from Spitalfields to Brixton. I had picketed power stations during the miners strike with a wind chill of minus eighteen. Was I really going to take seriously this backwoods two bit *petit bourgeois* opportunist hack? I wanted to talk issues comrade.

I warmed to my theme: 'But for example what is the your policy on getting a ceasefire from the IRA, and negotiating with the British Government on bringing peace to Ireland. And where do you stand on global warming?'

'No, no, no, forget about that,' said the candidate. 'What I'm asking is, what can I do for *you*? For instance, I just drove up this terrible track to your cottage. Can't I get it tarred for you?'

That shut me up. 'You could get this dirt track tarred?'
'Sure,' he said with a big grin, 'anything to keep our constituents happy.'

'How much will I have to pay?' I said thinking there must be a catch in this absurd offer

'Nothing at all, at all. Why sure, that's what you pays your taxes for isn't it?' he said. I wondered if the state thought it might make economic sense to spend one hundred thousand Irish punt on tarring a road that only I would use. It would certainly assist in getting to the dole office a bit quicker.

'I would very much like the road to be tarred,' I said.

'Is that all?' he said, 'You know we need to get everything on the list at an early stage so that no-one's disappointed.'

'Well, actually there is. I applied for a telephone some months back, and although I understand that it will be a huge capital outlay for Telecom Eireann in terms of poles and cables to get a line up here, we'd really like a phone.'

The politician waved his arms expansively: 'Roads, telephones - that's what you want, that's what you'll gets, that's our policy. Now don't you forget to go down to town next week on Wednesday and put your cross in that little box next to my face.' He grinned again.

'For a road and a telephone that would seem like a small price to pay,' I said as they got into the shiny car, convinced that another constituent could be marked off in their favour.

Ten minutes later we'd forgotten all about this surreal little visit. Imagine our surprise when three weeks later the politician - whose name I had not forgotten, because I could not recall noting it in the first place - sent us a letter with two enclosures. The first was from the CEO of Telecom Eireann to the Irish Minister of State for Communications assuring him that he was looking into our telephone application and the second was from the Minister himself. On a letterhead of the Office of the Minister for Tourism, Transport and Communications the Minister wrote:

Dear John,

I enclose an acknowledgment which I received recently from the Chief Executive of Telecom Eireann in response to my representations on behalf of Mr. Tim Haynes, Dromleagh, Beaufort, regarding his order for telephone service. I will be in touch with you again shortly.

Yours sincerely,

Seamus

Seamus Brennan T.D.

Minister for Tourism, Transport and Communications.

Two weeks after our receipt of this letter, workers moved in, sinking poles and pulling cable, and a month later we had a telephone.

'When was that election?' I said to Clare, knowing that whenever it was it had long since been and gone. 'It looks like my big cynical self underestimated the power of politics at the ballot box.'

I did give the local politician a call on our new telephone, informing him that the works had been executed and thank you very much.

'And so when do you think they'll be starting on the road then?' I asked mischievously.

He said something which sounded like 'sometime before the next election', but I couldn't be sure.

11. TURF WARS

Donal and Maire Houlihan kept themselves a little aloof from the rest of the valley folk. Unlike everybody else they didn't farm their own lands and they lived in a bungalow adjoining Donal's parents house. Donal managed a large, profitable farm belonging to a wealthy Irish contractor who lived in London. The farm was some miles away, outside the small village of Milltown. The land was flat and the fields large, providing rich pasture for the husbanding of sheep and cow alike. Donal looked after the flock of some 200 ewes, and turned over dozens of heifers a month to the abattoir in Cork. In addition he kept an eye on the palatial homestead, which included an indoor swimming pool. Donal used the company car, an impressive Mercedes 4 x 4. The Houlihans had a little more disposable income than most in the valley, and Maire used some of it on clothes and make up. Her usual footwear was a pair of trim court shoes, and only when she absolutely had to did she stoop to level of the rest of the valley low life and pull on a pair of wellington's, even though hers were white.

In turn, the Houlihan's were regarded as 'shnooty'. They even went to different pubs, or otherwise kept themselves to themselves. Both sides generally disregarded the other. For the first couple of years, because of their lack of participation in the valley's communal life, we didn't get to know them beyond a friendly salute as our car and theirs passed on the narrow lanes.

We needed turf to fire up our cast iron fire and water heater, and I became part of a turf cutting team on Seamus Sheehan's bit of bog, close to our cottage. The practice of turf cutting was dying-out. It was very hard work that relied on mutual cooperation. As cash got easier to come by, it was simpler by far to order in a load of coal than to toil away on the banks of a bog. People willing to assist with the laborious process were getting fewer and further between, and the weather which seemed to be getting wetter down the years, made the whole process increasingly burdensome.

The turf was cut by a man using a type of spade called a *slean*. A second person then piked the sods, flinging them onto the bank. A third person, also using a pike, then laid them out tidily on the bank to allow their upturned faces to dry out and develop a crust. The process would be repeated on the other side of the sod, weather willing. After some more dry weather, the sods would be turned onto their ends, and stacked together in groups of three or four. After still more dry weather, these little pyramids would be built into large *stoops* which would dry the sods, ready for transport by tractor and trailer or even mule and cart, depending on who and where you were.

In days of yore, whole families and communities would turn out on the banks of the bog and set themselves to the back-breaking work. Even today, it was an occasion for the locals to get together and in the time it took to get the sods onto the bank, they had ample opportunity to gossip about everybody and every happening in the locality.

Across the river from Seamus Sheehan's bank was Dinny Houlihan's bank, from which Maire and Donal, Dinny's son, cut their turf. Donal would hire someone to give him a hand to cut and pike, and it was Maire's responsibility to do the turning whenever the weather permitted. One summer's day I was toiling away with a couple of boyos on Seamus Sheehan's bank when we noticed that Maire was turning sods on the Houlihan's bank across the river. We had paused to catch our breath and the boys were standing around leaning on *slean* and pikes, discussing this and that. Then somebody said:

'And who might that be alone on Dinny Houlihan's bog?'

Everyone gawked into the distance and spotted Maire.

'What the fuck is that bitch wearing?'

'She's wearing a tight skirt, I can see that much'

'No but I'd swear she's working barefoot'

'Noo, impossible'

Everyone squinted hard.

'She's wearing them high heels'

'Noo, impossible'

'Oh yeah she is'

'A tight little skirt and high heels it is. In the bog. This must be a first in the history of the bog.'

And then the boys were off.

'In the fecking bog with high heels and a shkirt. Fucking crazy. So help me God. Who does she think she is, the fucking queen of the bog?'

'That *hoor* defies the law that you can take the man out of the bog, but you can't take the bog out of the man.'

'Too right, Seamus. She's taking the fecking piss out of the bog.'

'She's taking more than the piss out the bog, she's taking the whole fucking bog out of the bog.'
'There'll be no more bog by the time she's finished with it.'

'May God strike us all down with a fuckking feather.'

Poor, maligned Maire did look a sight squatting down on her haunches - the only possible way for her to get her hands to ground level with the little black heels and tight skirt. It must have been even harder work turning the sods in this way, but Maire's appearance out there, alone on the bog, was important enough to her to overcome any additional physical demand occasioned by her ridiculous outfit.

The boys discussed the Houlihans and their shnootiness, and rumors that Donal had made a right mess of his boss' farm and was soon to be fired. Then they were talking about other people in the valley, and in particular the bachelors and spinsters who were now getting on in years.

'And why hasn't Brid O'Sullivan escaped that devil father of hers and taken up with lonely old Finbar?'

'At leasht twould be a bit of company'

'At leasht they would keep each other a little warm at night'.

And the whole company started getting dewy-eyed about the lonely folk, and how they should get together and live happily ever after. And then somebody asked Packy Macarthy how was his missus, well knowing that she was an absolute dragon and that their marriage was a disaster.

'So, so' was all Packy would say, and then after a long, pensive silence by the whole gang, Packy piped up:

'Maybe the lonely folk in the valley should stay just the way they are.'

And everybody, silently contemplating their own domestic situations, nodded their agreement and started talking sadly about how great it would be to be all alone, all things considered.

'At leasht a man could go down and enjoy a pint in a bit of peace and quiet.'

The melancholy atmosphere brought on by tiring bodies and unhappy thoughts was broken by the distant sight of Sheila Sheehan briskly making her way towards the bog lopsided by a huge basket which the boys knew to contain a couple of loaves of bread value added by thin slivers of ham and thick wedges of cheese. To be washed down by a couple of huge flasks of tea. It was customary for the wife of the man of the bog to provide the mid-day nourishment.

Packy Macarthy uncurled his stiffening back into the vertical, spotted Sheila and said... 'Fuck it lads, I'm so hungry I could eat Chrisht off the cross.'

I was gobsmacked by this statement to such an extent that I thought I had misheard. But the retort that it occasioned informed me that there was no mistake.

'Well I might not be quite as hungry as you Packy, but I could still eat a nun's arse through a gate,' said Seamus.

The boys downed tools, found a soft patch of grass and settled down to the glorious feeling of tiredness, food in the mouth and eyes closing in the unusual luxury of the warmth of the sun.

Seamus Sheehan's bank was starting to look fairly lean, he consequently did not wish to sell me a trailer-load for our own consumption.

'But why not go and ask the Houlihans,' he suggested. 'Their bog is huge, they sell trailers to people every year and it's high quality turf,'

And so I went to visit the Houlihans. They were very friendly and we negotiated the sale of a trailer of turf, and delivery up to our cottage. They suggested that the following year I take a bank and cut it myself. I resolved to do just that.

The following year, I walked the bog with Dinny Houlihan and he pointed out which bank I could call my own. I asked whether he would be cutting that year, he said no, he would be trying the machine turf this time.

Spring was over and summer was getting into full stride when the rain broke sufficiently to allow me to contemplate a day's work in the bog. I hoisted the *slean* and pike on my shoulder, kissed the family goodbye and with my bag of refreshments, set off for a day's hard labour in the bog. It was a wonderful day. The rain is a permanent filter to the air, so when it stops and the sun shines there is no dust and no haze. Visibility was perfect, the landscape washed, clear, pristine. The air smelled sweet. That day Ireland was indeed emerald, a million subtle sparkles of the different shades of green.

I strolled down our lane through the lands of Dromleagh, past the hazelnuts, past the red berries of the mountain ash, the bright green of the new fern sprouts, the silver and wrinkled parchment of the birch. The world felt new and vital. The last sounds of the soon to be departed cuckoo whistled through the forest below the lane. The solid yellow gorse rose against the ageless granite of the hills of Macgillycuddy Reeks beneath the awe inspiring Mount Carrountoohil.

It was one of those days that made you feel good just to be alive. Ireland was great, and six months of ceaseless rain, storms and black skies were instantly forgiven. This is what it's all about, I thought, as I contemplated a day of simple productivity and aesthetic satisfaction.

I stopped on the stone bridge crossing into Gortloughcra. The bridge was a construction of hand-laid stones that had not been selected to fit the appropriate spot. The bridge had stood as long as anyone could remember, now every crack was filled with a creeper, lichen, moss or fern and spilled over the silver surface of the stream below. I could never walk past this spot without hopping down onto a rock and taking a draft of the sparkling water. It was like sipping earth's medicine, one could feel the coolness hit the stomach and spread through the body like a tonic, and I would feel wholly alive, strong, excited and satisfied.

As I turned off the lane and through the rickety, rusted farm gate of Dinny Houlihan's bog, I became aware of a humming machine in the distance. In my wellingtons, I tramped through the different banks of the bog to that which had been allotted to me. Finding a cool spot for my sandwich bag and flask of water just collected from the stream, I rolled up my sleeves and felt the handle of the slaun ready for that first sod of turf to be cut from my very own bank.

The hum of the machine was no longer a hum, it was a roar. Not fifty meters from where I was about to start cutting, was a huge mechanical digger with a front-toothed bucket that was taking bites from the bank much as a spoon would take a heap from a bowl. The digger would then move to dump the load into a trailer affixed to a tractor. The trailer boasted a huge corkscrew which was simultaneously mashing the turf and pushing it into a compressor, extruding the turf out its rear end onto the bank in perfect sods. For a while I stood marveling at this process. After a while, I sat down on the bank and laughed out loud at the ridiculousness of it all. Here was a blow-in, a foreigner, a city slicker, gone to the bog to cut his turf as the local people had done down the centuries in time honored tradition. Alongside me was a local, employing an embodiment of modern technology, to do the same. I felt like a Luddite about to be gobbled up by Franz Kafka's thresher.

With the unbearable whine of the machine in my ears and its fumes in my nose, I left the bog, knowing that this scene would be the subject matter of *craic* in the pub on the weekend:

'And there, in the middle of the bog, stands this one fecking blow-in, breaking his back at the cutting of the turf, while all around him the machine is spewing out those sods ten to the dozen to every one of his, and no effort at all, at all.'

'What harm, let the fecking foreigner cut his turf, its only costing him a sore back, ha ha ha.'

'No, it's costing him more than a sore back. What about the money he's paying Dinny Houlihan for the bank, ha, ha,ha.'

'And what about the money he's paying Donal Houlihan for the trailer to his house?'

'Then the Houlihans use that money to pay for the machine turf, ha,ha,ha.'

'So everyone's happy, ha,ha,ha.'

Clare and I visited South Africa, the country of our birth, at the end of that year. It was a visit to both our families, to show off our new addition to the family, Gina. Ciaran, growing by leaps and bounds, was keen to meet grandpas and grandmas, uncles and aunts - all things that everyone else had in Ireland and were so important, but that he didn't have.

The dates for the trip were carefully planned around dole days - to miss one and then have to sign on with all the attendant unpleasantness was not worth it. In the end it meant I returned to Ireland a few days earlier than Clare and the children.

We left the van in the yard of our by now good friends Maire and Donal Houlihan's yard, for safe keeping.

I returned from the holiday at eleven a.m. one bitterly cold early February morning. Snow covered the mountains. I knocked on the Houlihans door to let them know that I was back and would be returning later in the day to fetch the van. After a long interval, the door was opened a crack.

'Hi, Maire,' I said. ' I'm back.'

'Hallo,' she said, not giving an inch on the door.

'How are you?" I asked politely, while my extremities, nicely baked by African sunshine, froze up like fishfingers.

'Fine,' she said, 'wait there,' and so saying she closed the door.

I was confused, and put out.

A moment later she came outside, pulling on an overcoat and snapping shut the door behind her.

'Wait there,' she said again, and took off in the direction of the house next door. This was Donal's parent's house. Donal's brother, Christy and his wife and child of two also lived there.

Finally I began to grasp what was happening. Maire could not let me in, as the two of us would be alone in her house, foreshadowing another social disaster in the valley where, as I'd found out at the O'Sullivan's, the hills themselves have eyes. She had gone next door to try to get someone to join her, to make the situation socially acceptable, but she found no-one at home.

She returned looking confused and embarrassed.

'I'll lift you home' she stammered.

'No, I've got my car right here,' I said, stubbornly refusing to help her out.

'I'll bring your van up later' she tried again, now blushing bright red as well.

I turned to my car.

'See you, ' I said and slammed the door.

Yet again I was having difficulty with the rules of country social intercourse. How long might it take us to learn them and was it worth it? Increasingly it was becoming a problem. Increasingly I didn't want to think about it.

12. THE LAMBING

Through our connection over the turf, we had become acquainted with the Houlihans, Maire and Donal. Donal occasionally needed an extra pair of hands on the farm he managed for his boss in London. The farm was well mechanised, and the everyday running of it could be handled by Donal alone. However, certain functions required more than one pair of hands, and at times like these, he would call on people he knew who had free time at their disposal to give him some assistance. I became one of those people.

'Tim, I need some help with the lambing this year, could you help me out?' came the request over a Guinness in the pub one night.

'But Donal,' I said, ' I know nothing about sheep and lambs.' I didn't want to add that I was unsure of my capacity for blood and guts either.

'Why sure, don't you worry about that at all at all, any *eedjit* can pick it up in a minute as long as you don't mind a little blood and shite. Just bring your wellingtons, we don't need a veterinary surgeon, not before we start anyway.'

This sounded ominous. But I needed the extra cash, so I agreed to go with him the following day to acquaint myself with the farm, and what needed to be done.

The farm was indeed impressive. Its lush rolling fields were quite unlike the rocky gorse-studded lands of our impoverished foothills. The sheep were white, round and fat, their plumpness exaggerated by their late state of pregnancy. The house was palatial. From wide lawns we slid open the floor to ceiling glass patio doors, behind which rippled an indoor pool, a rare luxury in Ireland. Donal needed to get the filter working as some family members would be back from London that weekend. I asked Donal if he ever had a swim in the pool.

'No' he said, looking at me like I was indeed some kind of irresponsible *eedjit*,. ' I can't swim, nor would I want too. Yerrah, where is the sense in deliberately getting wet and cold and at the same time putting your life at risk?' he asked rhetorically. 'We spend enough time and money just keeping ourselves warm and dry.'

Then we were on the tractor and off to the huge barns which housed the heifers.

A spiked contraption was mounted on the front of the tractor. These spikes were driven into the silage, which was lifted into the barn and distributed down a central walkway between two rows of fenced in heifers. While Donal continued to bring in and dump silage, I spread the silage with a pike and mixed some special nuts into the feed. The heifers pushed their heads through the railings and chomped at the food. These animals were on the last lap of fattening ('finishing' was the word Donal used) before a final trip to the abattoir.

Having completed this job, Donal and I walked over to an even bigger barn in which there were large pens containing many different sizes, weights and ages of animals at various stages of beef production. I stayed out of the pens while Donal walked between the animals, prodding this one, inspecting that one, with a keen eye for sickness or injury. One animal took exception to Donal's inspection and turned its head as if to butt him. Donal went crazy.

'You fucking devil you,' he screamed at the animal, aiming first a kick at its hind quarters and then bringing down the handle of a pike on its head.

'We'll see who's fecking high and mighty when we go for our holidays at Cork next week, you fucking black cunt of a devil you.' The abattoir was at Cork.

The personal offence taken at the cow's behaviour, not to mention Donal's towering fury, was absurd. The incident was shortly forgotten, only to be startlingly resurrected a week later when Donal proudly announced that he had settled the score.

'What matter might you be referring too' I asked.

'You know, that black devil that attacked me lasht week in the shed' he said, 'Well, I personally walked him up the aisle at the abattoir, all the while telling him that he was about to go to hell and back, and then just before they put the bolt to his brain I gave him a right land across the eyes and told him that the likes of him should not be fucking with me.'

The absurdity was complete. I asked Donal if he always watched the animals that he'd brought to life and grown, put to death.

'Yeah, oh yeah' he said ' I always shtay until the knife does its work so that I can see the quality of the meat. You should come down with me next time, you'll love it down there.'

My introduction to the farm complete, we parted with Donal saying he'd call me as soon as the first lambs were on the way. The plan was that he would look after the business of the day, and I would be on night shift. But with two hundred lambs, others would be called in if necessary.

A week later, the call came. A few lambs had been born that day, so I should meet Donal at his bungalow (he'd returned for his evening meal) and we'd go over to the farm together after the tea.

The rain was bucketing down in the pitch darkness as the lights of the Mercedes 4x4 picked out the lane to the farm. We made a dash for what used to be stables. These had been made into snug compartments with bales of hay, and already a few ewes and their new lambs nestled in them. The bare bulbs lit up what resembled a happy nativity scene - all that was needed was Joseph, Mary, and the baby Jesus himself, to make the setting complete.

The end room had been set aside for deliveries, and the straw on the concrete floor was already laced with afterbirth and oozing red blood. There was one bewildered looking ewe, eyes rolling slightly, dashing back and forth between the bales of hay.

'Now let me show you what to do' said Donal taking off his Parka, and rolling up his sleeves. I did the same.

'Make sure you've got a bucket of water handy. You see that stuff hanging out the cunt, that means the waters have broken. You can see it's looking all puffy and tender, this means the lambs' ready to come.' In truth I couldn't tell that the cunt was all puffy and swollen, because I'd never paid one that much mind up until that point, but I observed closely and took Donal's word for it.

'Now, you force her into the corner like this, hold her tight with your legs, and stick your fingers in here and, if you can't see the front paws, you'll feel their tips. The head will follow just behind the front paws. If all is well, that is.'

Donal stuck his fingers in, found what he was looking for and urged me to do the same. I was feeling a little queasy, but fortunately I hadn't eaten for a while and I started a mantra in my head, something like 'a job is a job is a job...'

Donal could see that I was a little tentative.

'Yerrah, now Tim, don't you remember when the missus brought your beautiful young Gina into the world, it's the same bloody thing,' he urged sensitively.

'I didn't stick my arm in and drag her out by the front paws,

Donal,' I said, thinking that there had to be a more substantial difference that I couldn't put my finger on at that moment.

On the video screen in my brain, a picture appeared of a vaginal passage crowded with billions of gyrating sperm dots, racing towards that tiny seed further up the tunnel. Michelangelo's fingers on the ceiling of the Sistine chapel, about to paint that miniscule act of miraculous creation, the defining moment in all life as we know it, to grow from this molecule into an Einstein, a Mother Teresa, Jeffrey Dahmer, or an innocent lamb. I still couldn't put my finger on the difference, and I certainly wasn't about to engage Donal on the subject.

And then he had the front paws in his grip, with the head fast on the heels. He pulled and pulled until the bulk of the body burst through the mother's tight ring and squelched out in a bloody heap on the straw. It was covered in a membrane which had to be quickly removed so that the lamb could breathe. Then half a pail of cold water was thrown over the animal, which, after some beginners' attempts at standing, wobbled groggily up onto its legs. The ewe, fearful of the human presence, seemed indecisive until Donal jammed the lamb onto her willing teat. Not all ewes were so accommodating.

'Nice healthy little fella,' said Donal, rising to go and do his own ablutions, which consisted of washing the blood and slime off his arms and hands before midwifing the next one. There were one hundred and ninety nine still to go.

It has to be said that I held sheep in serious contempt. Often when driving my car up the lane to our cottage, I had come across sheep on the road, trapped between a wire fence running up one side of the lane and a steep stony bank on the other. I confess to keeping my foot on the accelerator to get them charging up the road ahead of me. After all of fifteen meters, the first one would give up and huddle against the wire fence with its eyes tight shut. To the sheep, the car represented the same danger as say, a fox, and therefore death was touching its shoulder. And its life force, its will to live, lasted all of a fifteen metre dash. Life might have been tough in them thar hills, but fifteen meters was a pathetic effort by any stretch of the imagination.

With everything momentarily under control in the delivery room, Donal suggested that we go into the field to check on whether any more ewes were ready to pop. We put on our NATO Parkas, and dashed through the rain to board the tractor, which fortunately had a glassed-in cab. The tractor pulled a small version of a horse-box, into which we could load the ewes. Visibility was so bad that even Donal temporarily lost the way crossing the few fields to the one that held the sheep. I hopped off the tractor into the mud and driving rain to open the gate. The tractor's headlights scanned the sheep, which were huddled together in small groups or lying on the ground with their feet tucked under them. They looked at us in that stupid sheep way. Then Donal pointed out a ewe standing away from the others, and moving in an agitated way. A glance at its rear end showed some dangling membranes dancing silver and scarlet by the tractor's bright light. Inexplicably, I thought of Nureyev and Fonteyn dancing Sir Frederick Ashton's 'Giselle'. Dame Margot is just arising from a delirious rest on her deathbed, imagining herself at a ball. Amid the misty-edged room glittering crystal white and silver, she stands resplendent in a scarlet ball-gown, receiving the attentions of would-be suitors. In strides Rudolf with his ghostly white muscles and handsome ballbag, and they dance passionately in the chandelier's light.

'Her waters have broke,' Donal announced gravely, wrenching me back from Rudolf and Margot to the ewe's rear end. 'We must get her in'.

We scanned the rest of the sheep and spotted another in a similar condition. Donal manouvered the tractor to isolate the lone ewe, then we both hopped out with torches, let down the back flap of the horse box, and set about coaxing her in into the box in a pincer maneuvre. Once in, we lifted the back flap and moved on to the next ewe. Drenched and mud-spattered, we drove them back to the labour ward. The first was delivered of her lamb without a hitch, but the second, although showing signs of increasing distress, seemed to have the lamb inside pointed in the wrong direction. This was Donal's diagnosis anyway, followed by a demonstration:

'Now, in a case like this you shtick your hand in here ...' He inserted his hand into the ewe's vagina. '... and make sure you get the right hole.' He said this seriously, as if it had happened to him that he'd stuck his hand in the wrong one. 'Then you feel for the front feet, put the two together, then find the head...but it might be a bit too slippery,' he says while he's working away, 'in which case, we'll need a rope.' Donal retrieved his arm.

'I'll go and get a bit of rope' he offered, 'why don't you shtick your arm in there and get a feel for it, but don't go further than your elbow, or else you would have gone too far.'

I couldn't do it. I guess if Donal had been there I would have, but with him out for a moment I was not going to chance making the same mistake that he must once have made. Besides, even if I got the right orifice, I might mistake the sheep's heart for the lamb's head, and yank the whole thing inside out. The sheep was breathing heavily, its eyes rolling at me with either stress or disdain, I wasn't sure which. Then Donal came back and I heaved a sigh of relief.

'Did you give it a go then?' he asked in a sing-song voice.

'Yes' I lied, 'but I couldn't find the feet.'

'Never mind,' he said, 'you'll be a proper old class of a vet by the end of the night, I can guarantee you that.'

I thought about my school days. In both junior prep and high school I'd been a star pupil. I was vice-head prefect, captain of the cricket team, in the first rugby team, popular with teachers and pupils alike. I was going to university. There existed for me a comfortably angled ladder to the top. I would be a captain of industry, an outstanding surgeon, a reputable politician, anything was possible. All that was required was for me to continue the steady tread, rung by rung up that ladder. Then something happened, a broken rung, a slip of the foot, a blackout causing a loss of grip. And to cut a long story short, here I was with a second, stirring chance to reclaim my true fate! By the rosy light of daybreak, I would be a vet.

Donal had brought a short piece of rope the end of which he formed into a knot that could be pulled tight around the feet. In went his arm with the rope, the other end of which trailed out onto the floor. He rooted about a bit in there, and while I was battening down the sheep with my knees, he started to tug on the rope. Two feet emerged, then the head, and then the rest of the lamb popped out.

'So that's about it then,' he said, with satisfaction. It was about ten o'clock in the evening. 'I'll go away and get some shleep and leave you to it. If you have any problems just go into the house and give me a call. It doesn't matter what time it might be, just call.'

He was gone. I was in control of a farm with two hundred sheep about to give birth after an apprenticeship of an hour. The craziness of it had me smiling, and then as is my natural propensity for paranoia, I began imagining what disasters could possibly befall me. It started with small things going wrong. In my minds-eye it got worse and worse until, eventually, I boarded the tractor which I got going but couldn't control. It careened across the yard, up the lawn in front of the fancy house and straight through the full length glass patio windows of the beautiful farmhouse and into the indoor swimming pool. The bleating of the ewes, already safely given birth and warm in the barn, brought me back to my senses, reminding me that I should revisit the top field to check for any new arrivals.

I boarded the tractor, got everything vaguely right on the controls and was off to the top field. Like Donal, I lost my way in the rain and spent a long time driving up and down alongside stone walls until eventually I stumbled upon the right gate. I trained the headlights on the sheep until I spotted one disturbed-looking animal and got up as close as I could. I hopped down from the cab and the ewe took off, I saw that the lamb's head was already showing.

Like all courses of instruction, the one I'd had in sheep gathering and birthing had not included this possibility. I had to use my own initiative to bring ewe and lamb safely back to fold. First I gave chase on foot, but she was too far ahead of me and I needed her back in the trailer anyway. Then I returned to the tractor and set off after her in diesel turbo. When I got close, the lamb's head was no longer there. Had she dropped the lamb on the way? In which case, I'd certainly run over it. Had the lamb seen the rain, me and the tractor and decided 'fuck this for a game of cowboys' and disappeared back inside? Could a lamb do that and still breathe?

I got close again in the tractor. The ewe was running out of steam. I took off after her on foot, brought her down and dragged her back to the box. I picked up another couple of ewes with waters broke and headed back to the maternity ward, my head dripping with cold water but feeling exhilarated from the chase.

By the time I got back and off-loaded, I was unable to distinguish one sheep from the other, so whichever had had the lamb's head preview up on the top field was now any one of three. The first lamb popped out unaided by me. I pulled off the membrane, stuck the bleater on the teat and went for the next. I thought I could see the ends of the paws so I stuck my fingers in gingerly and the warm, soft, bloody lamb flooded out into my arms. The third was a problem, clearly the ewe was struggling. I felt for the paws … no paws. I went in deeper, then squeamishly removed my arm and resolved to wait and see what would happen. If nothing did, I would give Donal a call.

I travelled backwards and forwards to the field ferrying sheep which popped without much difficulty, but that earlier ewe remained in the pen looking uncomfortable and a bit wild with fear. Eventually, I could stand it no longer, and at three in the morning I called Donal.

He arrived twenty-five minutes later with Christy, his younger strapping brother, who played football for the Laune Rangers reserves and once got a hiding from Strong Jim. He had more experience, strength and confidence in the pulling of lambs. So this was a last resort before the vet was called. A real vet.

Christy got down to work. The arm went in with the rope, the rope was secured to the feet, and now while two of us held the sheep he used all his power to pull – in vain. Donal and I simply could not hold the sheep firmly enough. Between the three of us that sheep was taking serious strain.

There was a stout steel bar affixed across the door just above head height. Christy tied a rope to each of the ewe's back legs, and between the three of us we hoisted her by the ropes over the bar with her head pointing down. Christy went in again, and replaced the rope on the lamb's legs in the womb, and all three of us tugged that rope over the bar too. The feet emerged but no amount of pulling was going to dislodge the rest. The ewe, now looking distinctly weak and ill, was lowered. The vet was summoned and arrived half an hour later. The rain had eased off, and while Donal fetched a floodlight from the barn, the vet spread his instruments over the bonnet of the car and Christy fetched some shears to cut the wool from the sheep's rear flank.

Dawn was breaking. The clouds were thinning enough for streaks of early morning light to line the sky between the gray. Sounds of a new day were beginning to rise from the fields.

Donal and Christy held the sheep, while the vet's scalpel went for the incision. I couldn't look and disappeared inside to busy myself with the other ewes and lambs.

Ten minutes later I heard some 'Ooohs' and 'arghs' and other noises of revulsion interspersed with Hail Mary's. I went out just as the vet was putting the final stitches to a massive gash, from belly to back, down the side of the sheep. And lying on the ground nearby was a form with eight legs, two heads and one body. A twin that had gone wrong. Donal called to me, 'Don't go near it, it's the divil!'. Even these hardened old farm hacks were affected by this aberration. They were crossing themselves and saying Hail Mary's to protect themselves from any devil power that might be wafting up into the atmosphere from this monster. There was still a slight movement from bloody heap. It looked like something from a b-rated horror movie. But its sudden squirming, describing the life it still had, left me feeling a mixture of revulsion and pity.

It wasn't long before Donal was mocking Christy. 'You had your hands in there fondling that little she-divil, you little divil lover you.' And Christy got more and more aggrieved that the piss should be taken out of him for doing a job that no-one else was prepared to do. Donal was deep in conversation with the vet when Christy picked up the aborted eight legged monster by a leg, swung it round and brought it down between Donal's shoulder blades. Blood splatted everywhere. Fortunately Donal was still wearing his rainsuit so the bloody form slid down to the ground - but not before Donal had shrieked with absolute horror. His terror did not stop him picking up the *divil* and wielding it like an Olympic hammer thrower across the yard at Christy, who had taken off at a sensible sprint.

The lamb(s) were eventually cast over the back wall to join a few others that were still born, or had died shortly after birth. These miracles of nature were now no more than a stinking mess that would have to be buried in a hole via the bucket of a front loader.

13. LOST ON THE SWINGS

Apart from putting the finishing touches to our own cottage, the bulk of the rebuilding was complete, and I had time – and need – to worry about where the next paying job might come from. Though I had done odd jobs here and there in the valley, mostly sprucing up houses for the all-important annual stations, there was no way I could make a living working in that small circle of mostly dirt poor people.

Clare and I made a decision. I'd have to get more involved in Killorglin where there was more money, more people and more work. I had made some pieces of furniture inspired by old Irish designs, adding a modern touch. I needed a place that might double as a workshop and retail outlet in the fashion of the quaint, craftsy homegrown movement that was becoming all the rage in that part of Ireland, relying on the growing tourist market. We knew a Dutchman who was making a fortune out of little painted ceramic models of Irish traditional houses, leprechaun figurines and other decorative kitsch. It figured that my wooden Irish furniture, settles, cradles and dressers would have the same kind of appeal and market.

So the hunt was on for an appropriate building in the town. And what better spot than over the road from the square on which everyone who visited town had to park their cars, and with the illustrious Allied Irish Bank as a next door neighbour? The building was a small, ivy-clad stone-cut church that had stood empty for many years. It was beautiful, and it boasted a magnificent view over the Laune river. It was perfect.

I set about tracking down the owners of the church who turned out to be Protestant. It was easy enough establishing who was responsible for such matters, namely the Anglican bishop in Munster. I paid a visit to the other still functioning Protestant church in Killorglin, and secured the bishop's details from a parishioner on whom I had to wait while she finished her prayers. I gave the bishop a call and he suggested I pay him a visit at his residence outside Milltown.

I arrived one cold and blustery morning soon after, and was hugely impressed by the shabby elegance of the house and grounds. Milltown is a tiny town, not worth stopping in except for the public dump where we deposited our rubbish every two weeks. The dump attracted hordes of crows that formed a croaking black mass in the skies above Milltown, especially over those properties with large nesting trees. The bishop's residence had several huge Scots pines in the garden. It was like something out of a Mervyn Peake novel, an observation confirmed when I was shown into the large Victorian residence by a woman who was dressed like a cross between a nun and a tea lady at the school tuck shop.

I was ushered into an entrance hall off which stretched long passages stopped at the ends by closed doors. The heating system either wasn't on or wasn't working. It was cold and draughty. The rooms had beautifully ornate skirtings, cornices and ceilings, and shutters in boxes alongside the sash windows. When it was built it had clearly been fit for a … bishop. Now the place was falling apart with not even the pretence of adequate maintenance work. The shabbiness needed substantially more than a coat of paint to overcome it. I speculated that at some time the floors must have been magnificent. Now they were covered in tatty carpet or old-fashioned lino, through the holes or at the edges the tiny patterned tiles beneath were just visible.

I waited in the hall until the man himself appeared. He was large and bulbous, with an enormous, hairy mole growing out of his neck. I was so conscious of not allowing my eyes to stray to his incredible growth that concentration on the matter at hand was almost impossible. Bishop Boyle was wheezing, and there was a grey tinge to his jowls that made him seem ill. He wore a simple white robe with a huge cross chained around his neck. I imagined a great invisible lead from that neck chain to the Almighty himself. I thought of the Bishop more as a long-suffering sheep dog having to listen to the tedious woes of one of his flock, rather than as the shepherd. It might be necessary for him to offer some form of assistance in an absolute emergency, but a good bite on the arse would usually do the trick. Being a Protestant bishop in staunchly Catholic Ireland can't have been suffused with job satisfaction.

I had to remind myself what I was there for, and given my contempt for sheep, my attitude oscillated between refusing to act like one of the flock by talking to him as an equal, and reminding myself that I was indeed in search of sympathy, if not outright charity. I tried to emphasise the win-win nature of his renting out the church to me, while he kept stressing that it was a win for me and a pain in the butt for him, though not in so many words. The meeting closed on a sceptical note with both of us promising to return to our constituencies, he to his Church Council, and I to rejoin the rest of the flock in the valley.

In the following weeks I surveyed the church and made plans for the necessary renovations. I met various members of the 'church council' who demanded to know every detail of my plan, especially when it came to how much money I was going to spend and whether I had it. I began to get annoyed and pointed out that the church couldn't be that interested in the building's upkeep when they had watched it falling down for twenty years. In between these meetings, I continued to chat with the bishop himself, who liked to refer everything to the church council when clearly he was in complete charge.

Matters came to a head when I called him one morning and was summonsed to his office at 11am the following day, the one day and time of the week I couldn't go because I would be standing in the dole queue. Naturally I couldn't tell him this, so I said I was phoning from London where I had been forced to go on urgent business, and I wouldn't be back till Monday.

On Monday I called him and he said that the Church Committee were not keen to give me the building, but that he thought that he could change their minds.

'And how will you be able to change their minds?' I asked naively.

'Well, ahem,' he said, in an uncharacteristically hesitant tone, 'It's about your children. If you will send them to the little school we have in Castlemaine - they need a bit of help making up the numbers, for the government education grant you know - then I'm sure the committee might be persuaded to let you have the church. They might even be able to assist in the renovation.'

This took me by surprise, not least because we had never spoken about my personal circumstances. Clearly he had had his troops check me out, and was excited about the prospect of landing another Protestant soul in the numerically swamped Catholic Republic. As if we didn't have enough problems with integration as it was. The answer was a loud no, but I thought I would give the ball one final whack into his court.

'I don't have any children,' I lied.

There was a moment's silence on the line before the bishop sighed, 'Ah, such a pity then.'

And that was the end of my dealings with the church and the Church.

This initial forage around the town had not made us any friends, quite the opposite, if anything. About this time a notice appeared in the local paper, *The Kerryman,* announcing a meeting to be held in Killorglin for people interested in participating in the building of a childrens' playground. Seeing this as an opportunity to get involved with the inhabitants in a meaningful way, I resolved to go to the meeting.

There were ten people at the inaugural gathering, held in one of the quieter pubs, and none of the ten was a sheep farmer. They represented a range of Killorglin townsfolk: a civic minded teacher from the local college, an energetic doctor, a woman from the housing estate, the owner of several shops, a rep from the government employment incentive scheme office, a civil engineer and a councilor. Pretty much everyone, in fact, capable of implementing the plan for a playground in the town, except a builder. Which is where I came in.

Much of the groundwork had already been laid. A piece of derelict council land had been set aside by the local authority, play equipment catalogues had been obtained, and various agencies and individuals had committed finance. What was needed now was for someone to drive the physical process of putting the scheme together. It was perfect for me and the assembled luminaries offset the fact that I was a blow-in with the reality that there was no-one else. Not without a wrestle, the blow-in eventually got the thumbs up.

There were insufficient funds to go out and buy playground equipment from a big supplier, so it was proposed that the committee either raise more money or consider the cheaper option of designing and building an 'adventure playground' using logs, pipes and other natural materials. The second option would necessarily involve getting the townsfolk to provide free labour. As it was a project to benefit the whole community, it seemed fitting that the whole community might be involved in the process. The shop owner, the doctor, the engineer looked at the woman from the estate who promised that come the hour, the people from the estate would be there.

The committee was delighted. The second proposal made sense, the plans were approved and all assured me that I need only mention the day, time and task, and the entire town would be rallied to lend a hand. I located the logs at a state forest timber mill in County Clare some seventy miles away, and called Tommy Boon for advice on transporting them back to Killorglin.

'I've got a new truck,' he said.

I told him we'd need more than a little truck. This increased his enthusiasm, not being one to be discouraged by scale.

'I'll put the trailer on the back then.' Two days later he arrived to pick me up in a tiny, beat-up Toyota flatbed with an immense four wheeled farm tractor trailer on the back.

'Bejesus Tom, are you sure about this boy?' I said rather anxiously and noticing that I too was now employing some Kerry-speak.

'Git in, git' he said and we were off.

On the drive up to the timber mill I outlined the project to Tommy who was fascinated by the idea of the townsfolk coming out to help.

'And you won't be paying them?' he asked incredulously.

'No,' I said, 'it's for the benefit of all the people whose kids will have somewhere to play.'

'I dunno where you came from before you came here,' said Tommy 'but it must have been fucking toy town, where people come out to work for nothing? The people who own the fecking town on yer committee don't need no playgrounds, and as for the rest, if it's a choice between sitting in a nice cosy pub kicking the fecking kids crawling under the table or slaving away in the cold and wet for nothing, what do you think they'll chose?'

'I'm the blow-in, you tell me what they'll chose.'

'You're building that playground yer fucking self brother, that's what you're doing.' said Tommy, and we went on to discuss the all Ireland final and how Kerry were still in with a shout.

We arrived at the saw-mill and proceeded to load the logs. The immense trailer was rapidly filled, and the flat bed then took a few more logs. There remained a huge pile to be loaded.

'What do we do now?' I asked Tom.

'Keep loading boy,' he said

'You're the doctor,' I said sceptically.

A few more logs were loaded onto the trailer, then a few more on the truck. Then a few more on the trailer, then back to the truck. The wheels of the trailer and the truck were now bulging out at the sides like half flats. And still Tommy found space for another log here, another there.

'Now how the fuck is this thing going to go?' I eventually burst out.

'She'll go alright Maybe a little shlow, but she'll go. What I'm thinking is, how the fuck is she gonna shtop,' he said giving me a big wink.

The logs were on, tied high above the cab of the truck. We moved off slowly, and on the slightest bend in the road the truck lurched over on its collapsing tyre walls, on each little lump in the road the steel of the wheels would hit the tar. But this was just the type of challenge Tommy relished, seventy miles of it.

At a maximum speed of twenty five miles an hour, I figured the journey would take over three hours, so I nestled down in the seat and shut my eyes, only to conjure up visions of all the hills we had to go up, and, more nightmarishly, down.

I was thrown to the side in the cab as Tommy suddenly turned at right angles to the main road. We were in the middle of a small town.

'What's up?' I asked him, fearing the worst.

'The fecking guards,' he said, ' if they see us in this, we're dead."

'So you can see the guards in their little car, but they can't see us under these logs? And if they do spot us, we'll make a dash for it? Is that the plan?'

'You can take the piss, but they didn't see me that time,' was his response as he checked the rear view mirror.

Outside the town there was a mountain over which the road passed. It was a two mile climb to the top then a two mile steep drop to the bottom. It was already dark. We were down to fifteen miles an hour on the speedometer, the needle was shivering as if in fear.

'Has that trailer got its own brakes?' I asked, giving my panic away.

'No trailer's got its own brakes, but if its stopping that's worrying you, you could always shtick your wellingtons through the floor and brake on the road,' Tommy said with a manly laugh.

I took my foot off the hole in the floor and watched the

road passing under the truck. I mentally resolved that at thirty miles an hour exactly, I would fling open the door and dive out.

We reached the apex of the hill and the strained whine of the engine eased off for a short while across the flat. Then the noise I had been dreaming about for two hours started building. Tommy was using the engine to hold back the load. We were in second gear, and the whine was growing louder and higher. Then Tommy would hit the brakes, and the speed would reduce until the brakes were at burning point, then he'd release the brakes and the whine would continue building. Fifteen miles an hour, twenty, twenty three. Back to twenty. Twenty three, twenty five. The engine now sounded as if it was about to burst, right there in the cab between the two of us. Twenty five, twenty eight. I looked at the handle of the door, then at Tommy. He was concentrating hard. I was contemplating my evacuation: maybe a broken arm or leg at this speed, not worse. Twenty nine. The engine was screaming.

'Tommy, is this thing going to hold it?' I shouted above the engine.

'No problem,' he mouthed back, but without a smile.

The sound had stabilised. We were a long way down the hill. A few more minutes and the road began to flatten out. A town lay ahead, its lights beckoning through the black outside. Another few minutes and we passed the first building on its outskirts. We stopped at the first pub we saw. The truck was wheezing and hissing and smelling of burnt rubber. Tommy had a big grin on his face.

'You shat yourself, you bastard,' I said to him. He said nothing but his grin broadened.

The logs were rolled off the back of the truck and trailer at the yard of the derelict national school that I had managed to hire for the purpose of constructing the playground apparatus.

The land for the playground was wet and boggy. The topsoil had to be removed, and drainage pipes and a fill of round stones laid to create a dry, child-friendly surface on which to erect the play pieces. A local man and his earth-moving machine had been hired to do the job. While he got on with his work, I got on with mine, cutting, drilling and shaping the logs into balance beams, swings, chain walks, tunnels and ladders.

At every committee meeting I asked that the promises made about assistance now be realised, but not a soul or more importantly, a body, made an appearance at the playground.

'As soon as you're on site where everyone can see you they'll be there,' I was assured by the committee.

The earthworks at the playground site were complete, as were the log objects at the school workshop. Once again I was forced to call Tommy Boon to come and help me take them to the site.

As we loaded up, I knew what was coming.

'Where's all the help you were going to get from the town?' Tommy asked with a wide, mocking grin.

'You tell me,' I said, squirming.

'I already told you, you big eedjit.'

'We're going to have a big workday on Saturday,' I said once again knowing that all I was doing was keeping Tommy amused. I hardly believed in that possibility myself anymore.

At the next committee meeting I asked once again for

assistance to be mobilised. I spoke to the woman who came from the housing estate. Yes the men would definitely be there on Saturday. I spoke to the doctor. Yes he had already put out the word to all his patients who were now cured and they would all be out on Saturday. I spoke to the lady from the creche. Yes all the parents would be there on Saturday. I spoke to the man who owned and ran the chemist and supermarket. Yes all his customers had been notified that Saturday was the day. By the end of the meeting I was concerned that there wouldn't be sufficient jobs to do or tools to execute them with.

Saturday arrived. The local townsfolk scurried up and down the road bordering the playground, some on foot, some in cars, some pushing prams. But everyone seemed to suffer the same malady. A communal stiff neck precluded anyone form glancing sideways into the playground. Fortunately, having built our house out of huge stones single-handed, I was experienced at shifting large, heavy objects without assistance. Slowly the vertical logs were rigged into position, the horizontals were bolted into place, the chains were hung, the swing and slide bases were concreted in.

There was one further motivation for me to work away all day without complaint: I wouldn't have a chance to return to my van and drive home until very late that afternoon.

A few weeks earlier I had been stopped by the 'white squad'. The white squad were the dreaded customs police. I had been driving my English registered van on the roads of Kerry for four years. This was highly illegal. Any car from across the water had to be immediately registered in Ireland, the obvious object being to control the movement of vehicles between the two states and the illicit purchase and sale of English cars *sans* customs duties and tax. The white squad were much talked about and feared in our valley on account of their formidable search and seizure powers. It was only a miracle that it had taken them so long to catch up with my car. Having done so, I was cautioned that unless the Irish registration was completed immediately I would be in deep trouble. I was risking confiscation of the vehicle. They probably only let me go on account of my strange accent.

However, on that Saturday as I was building the playground I spotted out of the corner of my eye the white vehicle of the white squad parked on the bridge into Sunhill. The occupants were observing me closely. I remembered a pub conversation I had had with someone about the terrible white squad, the someone had said that they could only take action if you were caught actually inside the vehicle. Whether or not this was true, I worked away that Saturday without break, I never found reason to return to the car even though all the doors were open. A light shower came down, and I just got wet. I put that playground together like there was no tomorrow. I would have worked through the night if needs be, but fortunately as dusk began to fall, I heard the white squad motor come to life and the vehicle drifted away into town. I carried on for another hour, in case it was a ruse to get me into the van. I even made a few feints towards the van, but seeing no returning headlights I took to the driver's seat and got out of town like a bat out of hell.

The following week, a Friday it was, the playground was finished. A woman with a small child came over to me and asked if the children could play now.

'Let them play,' I said, thinking about Marie-Antoinette when she said 'let them eat cake'.

Within fifteen minutes the playground was full. There were children tearing around like mice in an experiment - falling, fighting, screaming, laughing, crying. The older kids had already colonised the swings and the slide, the teenagers had holed up in the concrete tunnels with their fags, the mums were standing around chatting and rocking babies in push-chairs.

I packed the last of my tools in the van and left, pleased that it was over. By any stretch of arithmetic, my attempts at insinuating myself in the town to secure more permanent employment, would have to be marked F for Failed.

14. TO KILL A MOCKINGBIRD

Within a few days of moving into our cottage at Dromleagh, Biddy Boon arrived with two large cardboard boxes on the back seat of her car. She had us take out the wobbling boxes from which came strange scratching noises, and announced coyly that we held in our arms our 'house warming' present. The boxes were opened to reveal three white hens and a cock. This description is more than a little complimentary. Rather, there flapped two dirty white hens, the third a red-fleshed monster with only a few chest feathers and one eye. The cock was the meanest looking son of an egg you'd ever be likely to see. What made them all even more unattractive was their size. They weren't cute little bundles of fluff, they were absurdly big, more the size of a small Christmas turkey. Even Ciaran, ever desperate for company and new diversions of any description, took one look at them and disappeared to continue his game of rearranging stones.

For Biddy, clearly this gift had killed two birds with one present. She sang the egg-laying praises of the hens before pointing out that they were also just ripe for the table - the choice was ours, whatever our preference. I knew that the reason we had been given them was because they were long past their eat-by date, Biddy knew that even big Joe would rather she splash out on a new little hen at O'Grady's supermarket than take the trouble to twist their considerable necks.

I hastily cobbled together a wire cage with a corrugated

iron roof, which had to be reinforced against attack by the dreaded fox. Over the ensuing days and weeks we watched in horror as the cock mounted the featherless hen – his talons buried in her raw back, his beak fastened onto what was left of the hen's comb - and humped away like a demented wretch. *Was this the cocks response to being hen pecked? If so, it seemed quite incommensurate.*

While these daily assaults continued, the eggs mounted up. Soon all the little bowls, and some big ones on the kitchen shelves were full of eggs. We couldn't remember which were the oldest, which the newest or which might by now be rotten. We hardly ate eggs, anyway, so we'd end up throwing out the lot. They kept coming all the same.

Ciaran, who was three at the time, couldn't stand to be near the birds. 'Why's he hurting that hen?' he would ask as the cock mounted a fresh attack on its featherless victim. An answer like 'that's how they make chickens' could easily result in his developing all kinds of psychological quirks and trauma if one believed in causal psychological development. 'Because that cock's a mean horrible bully,' was the answer he got, which individualised the matter and seemed far less capable of producing general damage. I mean, all cocks aren't like that are they?

I started looking in books with quaint titles like *Old days, old ways* for the best way to kill a cock. We were, after all in the country and this sort of thing must happen all the time. I asked around, and everybody said more or less the same thing. 'Just break the neck with a quick shake' or 'Hold them between your legs, a little slit on the throat and bleed them ready for the pot'. I remembered a film called 'La Comb, Lucien' where the fascist brute of the title catches a hen in the farmyard and with one blow of his fist knocks the head across the farmyard. I remembered when I was a child and went to the market with my mother and her friend who bought a live hen. Back at the house the head was lopped off with a small kitchen hatchet, and the body charged round the garden spurting blood for several minutes. None of these options seemed attractive.

While still dithering, I was forced into radical action.

In a fit of wild orgasmic delight one day, the cock took out the featherless hen's remaining eye. Worse still, it wasn't as if the eye had simply disappeared. It was hanging by a thread halfway down the red bird's neck. Both the hen and the cock had to go, and go immediately, before further brain damage was inflicted on Ciaran.

The hen seemed to sense that I was after her with evil intent, for although at best her vision was limited to bouncing glimpses of the sky and ground alternately, she took off whenever I got close enough to wrap my gloved hand around her neck. She worked me up into quite a sweat before I cornered her and dragged her off by the wings.

I had made sure that Clare kept Ciaran well away from being able to witness the cock's victim about to be taken out by an even bigger cock. Surely the knowledge that the world was an unjust place could wait until Ciaran was a bit older.

I found a spot away from the house hidden in the ferns and gorse and took a firm grip of the neck in my hands like a Chinese bangle, and twisted it. I expected to feel a little snap, and see the bird descend into peaceful sleep, never to be molested again. Instead the hen lashed out with its substantial drumstick legs making it quite clear that there would be no willing acceptance of this charitable execution. I broke out in a fresh sweat and tried again with an even more violent shake, still to no avail. Clearly, I had the wrong technique. Surely I should be able to do this instinctively. Surely humans should automatically know how to kill a bird so that they could eat, so that we could survive as a race? These thoughts weren't providing answers, but my brain finally reminded me that the bird needed air, not only to fly in, but also to breathe. So I tightened my Chinese bangle grip, bent my weight to the neck again at ninety degrees and pinned it to a rock. The hen gradually changed from red to blue, and the after a while all motion ceased.

I was not confidant that I could execute the same trick with the cock, but I had a far more ingenious idea. Entitled 'let nature take its course' the plan was as follows. I would simply chase the cock up the mountain behind the cottage to within the vicinity of the fox's lair and leave it there.

I returned to the cottage in time to see the cockerel aboard hen number two, cranking up my determination several notches. I put hand to a big stick and started ferrying the cock out the front gate and along the track leading towards the mountain. At first the cock looked at me quizzically, stuck out its haughty chest and moved along at its own pace. When it slowed, I would make to prod it with the stick whereupon it would squawk and strut arrogantly forward. When I wished it to turn off the track and up the mountain it cunningly doubled back past me, and sprinted back to the yard. I arrived home, out of breath, to see the cock humping the hen. Beside myself with rage, I tried to muster a false smile of self-irony when I saw Clare and Ciaran howling with laughter. Of course, they weren't the only ones watching. Across the valley and through the hole cut in the fuchsia bushes so were the O'Sullivan family, and God alone knows who else besides.

This time I prepared properly for that cocky cock's tricks, and though he again made several attempts to pass back around me, I thwarted them all. At last the cock was high on the mountain and looking lost. I couldn't help letting loose a last volley of pebbles before making my way back down the mountain, turning around frequently to make sure I wasn't being followed.

The next day I was stunned to hear Ciaran call: 'Dad, he's eating that hen again'. Sure enough there was the cock, body a-quiver, astride one of the hens. I broke up the party with my wellingtons, retrieved my stick and we were off again with me resolving that this time, dead or alive, that cock would not be back. For two hours I pushed, prodded, badgered, guided, beat and chased that cockerel through fields of fern and gorse, through valleys of forest, over stony ground, up high rocks, through stretches of bog and over streams until I knew that even I was going to have difficulty finding my way home. This time victory had to be mine.

Then I returned and told the family.

As had become my custom, I walked out of the cottage in the early morning before breakfast to sample the weather, the fresh air and check out what havoc the inevitable rain storm might have wreaked. One morning I was surprised to find the roof of an outbuilding lying beautifully intact in the middle of the front lawn. There was simply no end to the amount of tying down one had to do to combat the gale that regularly blew down (and sometimes up) the valley

This morning the weather was overcast, but calm with a light drizzle. It was one of those dull days when a gray pessimism descends on mood and temper, because prospects for improvement are zero. I went to look at a tree that had blown over in another recent storm, just off the track. As I gazed down the valley towards the uprooted tree, a sharp movement caught my eye. The wire fencing was jerking up and down - something was caught in it forty yards from where I was standing. I scampered onto some rocks to get a better look, and saw the body of a sheep lying on its back. It was wedged between a couple of rocks with its legs pointing skyward. On leg had been caught in the top wire of the fencing as the animal had tried to jump over.

At first I thought the red colour on the wool was the marking dye used to establish ownership, but as I got nearer I realised I had not been the first to notice this helpless creature. The crows had been there first. Its eyes had been removed and none too delicately either. It was horrible, just lying there jerking, wedged between the rocks, empty eye sockets shedding tears of blood. While it was probably near death, I felt I had to end its agony as quickly as possible. I remembered that years earlier I had found an almost dead bird which had been mutilated by a cat. Deciding on that occasion to end the bird's misery I couldn't work out the best way of doing the job. I ended up hitting it with the flat back of a shovel on some gravel in the back garden. The bird seemed to quiver a little, then blood fell out of its eyes like tears. It was awful. Those little red tears were still with me, only now to be replaced by the much larger ones of the sheep.

At the time I resolved that if ever there was a next time I would ensure that the method was more efficient. This was the next time and the question was how to kill an upturned sheep with no eyes stuck on a fence. The neck was ideally positioned for cutting but there was no way my constitution could deal with dragging a blade across it. A blow to the neck I could stomach. I ran back to the cottage to get my short hatchet, which had recently been sharpened. I stepped into the quiet house where the rest of the family slept on. For the first time in my life before breakfast, I took a big slug of John Power whisky straight out of the bottle.

Jogging back down to the sheep, I arrived just ahead of another family of crows. A quick heavy blow with the machete should do it. I positioned myself to avoid what I imagined would be the fountain of blood that would follow the blow.

I swallowed hard, breathed deep and let fly with the hatchet, only to have the tool bounce back off the thick matted and sodden woollen neck. The hatchet sprang back almost as fast as the blow had been delivered, and nearly smashed me in the face. There was no perceptible reaction from the sheep, it just carried on quivering. Another nightmare had begun, but like the little bird saga there was no turning back. Having no plan 'b', and being in no state to sit down and work one out, I let fly with a succession of mad blows, eventually making progress through the wool and leather. I was like Jack Nicholson gone berserk in The Shining. When I finally stopped to catch my breath, I realised the head was almost off. The sheep continued twitching, totally unappreciative of the service I had just rendered at great personal cost. There was nothing more to be done. Another sheep's carcass would litter and pollute the countryside with its stink while it was slowly devoured by crows, foxes, minks and finally maggots.

I walked back to the cottage, bloody machete in hand, feeling a bit light headed. I sat down and had another slug of whisky, just as the first of the family groggily rose from bed to wish me 'good morning'.

Perhaps it is a little unfair to mention Finbar Feneran in the animals section of this book. His animals do get a mention in this story, for the rest, the reason will become self evident.

Finbar was a chronic alcoholic. He always had been. It wasn't like it developed as a way of coping after a tragic incident in his life. It wasn't like his life as a forever citizen of that valley had been any harder than anyone else's. He was simply born to be an alcoholic. There were two factors that may have assisted in his confirmation into the high church of imbibe.

One, his older brother owned a pub in Killorglin. Two, like so many others in Ireland, Finbar had inherited money from a deceased relative who had done well in America.

So Finbar behaved like a sheep farmer. Sheep in various stages of decay and in ever dwindling numbers hung out on his land while he was in the pub. He was permanently in the pub. It often happened that he never came home at all. He would sit on his lonely stool, up at the counter under the blaring TV, with mostly only the publican to pass the time with. The publican was once heard to boast that to make a decent living he required only one patron, Finbar. And if for some strange reason Finbar was at home and didn't put in an appearance, the publican would go and fetch him. Finbar was a happy enough soul, for him it was just as good a way of existing as any other that he knew about or was prepared to try. The astonishing thing was, he appeared to require little else to sustain him. He ate nothing, trusting that there was enough sustenance in twenty five pints of Guinness a day to keep him alive and healthy. He was probably right. Very occasionally he would be visiting a neighbor and, as was custom, the woman of the house would put a big 'fry-up' on the table, only to have Finbar, embarrassed, push it to one side. Everyone had a soft spot for Finbar Feneran.

It's difficult to find one word to describe his house, several are necessary. It was an old stone cottage just off the road. Everything was battered, broken and falling apart. But the cherry on the top was that, as a sheep farmer, he had a few dogs, which were locked in the house when he was occupied elsewhere. The dogs' permanent residence inside the house produced several nasty results: they were mad and sick and the house was disgustingly filthy. Driving past Finbar's house, the frightening face and bared teeth of one of the dogs, snarling at a cracked window, would always make me press my foot a little harder on the accelerator.

About once a year Finbar would decide to clean up his act. Instead of heading off to the pub, he would be up at dawn, let out the dogs and walk down the valley trying to identify and gather what was left of his flock of sheep. On one of these rare and pointless days of rest for his poor kidneys, I met him on the track outside our cottage. The dogs were visibly enjoying being outdoors, but the appearance of one of them was horribly bizarre. It had no hair whatsoever. Finbar noticed my appalled gaze.

'The bitch has a little mange,' he said calling her over and giving her hairless body an affectionate cuddle.

'I gave her some shtuff to clear it up,' he continued, as if to explain what a caring and considerate animal lover he was.

By midday Finbar would begin to feel a little lonely out there with only a couple dogs to talk to. What harm if he just stopped in to the pub to see what was up with the fellas? And that would be the end of Farmer Finbar's great outdoors for another year.

One cold and wet winter's evening he was called home to discuss some 'business' with a couple of local farmers from the next valley who knew about Finbar because they too had common grazing rights on Mt. Carrountoohil. 'The boys' did not want to meet Finbar in the pub, as the nature of their business was private. Finbar brought in some logs and set a fire in the huge grate, pulled up some old rattan chairs and produced a few bottles of Guinness from a holdall brought from the pub, to show that he was a man of manners and class. He needn't have bothered, because the boys arrived with enough alcohol to ensure that any obstacle to agreement on the business at hand could be overcome.

With a huge fire roaring, the men's Parka jackets drying over the chair backs and the Guinness bottles opened, the formalities were begun. How's the weather been on this side, a bit different from that side, and not like last year ... Finbar mentioned 'this global warming thing' that he'd seen on the TV and that meant more rain and maybe the sea will come up the Laune river a bit. Finbar waxed lyrical about the spud and how conditions were not good anymore for growing in Ireland. He'd heard that they now imported spuds from Italy. Can you imagine, the Irish eating spuds from Italy? The World Cup football had just finished, but it hadn't yet lost its gloss as a topic of conversation. Finbar had seen more games on his reserved pub stool than anyone else. But the topic ended on a sad note.... how 'Packy Bonner kept us in, only to be put out by that fecking Italian Scalatachi. We buy their fecking shpuds AND they put us out the World Cup. There's no fecking democracy anymore.'

And the boys kept the bottles open and the tumblers full. Finbar, nearest the fire on his favourite three legged stool was heard to remark 'if it was good enough for my father and his father before that, it's good enough for me'. He was starting to look a little jaded and weary. The boys passed meaningful glances at each other and the real business was broached before it was too late.

'This fecking ol' sheep farming has become a right ol' yoke these days, a lot of work, and not much money,' was the opening gambit from one of the lad's.

'And the cost of the nuts, and the dip? You have to sell the coat off your back to pay for it," said Finbar, proud to show that he was up with these things.

'And then there's the shearing, what that can only do to the back of a man,' said another of the lad's.

Finbar nodded: 'And the lambing doesn't get any easier.'

'And when was the last time there was an increase in the grant money?' said one of the boys, finally arriving at the real business.

'Only the big feckers can survive on it now, cause you need the numbers to make it worth the money,' said Finbar.

'Quite right, Finbar, well said boyo,' said the boys pouring fresh draughts all round. Finbar's eyes were half closed, he was swaying a little on his stool. More logs were thrown on the fire, the coals of which were so hot that fresh flames immediately sprang to life.

'But we can beat these big boys at their own game, we just have to work together on this,' said one of the boys. But Finbar's mind was no longer on the matter at hand.

'Eh, Finbar, Finbar?' One of the lads gave him a land across the back, bringing Finbar back to life.

'As I was saying Finbar, we have to work together on this. We can do this by putting all our sheep together into one pool, to make up the numbers like. And there's money in it too, y'know. We could give you a handsome price for your sheep quota. That way we'd be doing all the hard work, and you could start to take the weight off your feet a little like.'

But the business proposal fell on deaf ears. Finbar was fast asleep, finely balanced on his little stool in front of the red-hot fire.

'Fucking asshole,' said one of the lads, as they rose to put on their coats

'Waste of time and good beer money. Fucking asshole alcoholic.'

They threw the door open and bent their heads into the icy wet blast outside. But before they had settled into their car there was a roar from the house and a red glow, and they turned to see the doorway blocked by an apparition from a horror movie. Finbar was on fire. He stumbled outside and fell into the wet gravel and grass. The boys sprang from the car, ripping off their coats and flinging them over Finbar, then rolling him on the wet ground.

When the flames were doused Finbar lay smoking on the ground. He was groaning, and even by the light of the door it was clear that his hair was gone, the side of his face and ear were black, and his hand and arm were a mess.

'Put him in the car. We better drop the silly fecker at the hospital,' said the boys with disgust. The evening had ended most unsatisfactorily.

Maire Houlihan called Clare to ask if she was interested in accompanying her to an exercise class that had just been started in the village hall at Beaufort. Clare was only too pleased to avail herself of a chance to get out of the house and have the monotony of the company of two small children broken, albeit very temporarily.

There was a motley crew of women at the Beaufort village community hall that day, with Maire Houlihan, who removed her heels and peeled down to a pink leotard before slipping into matching leggings, resembling a Baywatch babe by comparison to the rest of the class which comprised of the grey and misty women of Beaufort. While Maire was a world apart in terms of glamour, the other end of the scale was represented by a woman who resembled, in shape, the wobbly man from Noddy and in the fashion sense, any one of the women from a Mad Max movie except Tina Turner.

'Who's that?' Clare whispered behind her hand to Maire as the unlikely dance troupe started marching round the hall with 'Lily the Pink' blaring horribly from a scratched record player. The 'Mad Max' woman was marching in the opposite direction from the rest of the class, and even though the instructor was a disciple of the dragon school of discipline, she allowed this one errant participant complete freedom of expression.

'Finbar Feneran's sister,' Maire Houlihan grimaced.

Finbar's sister whose name, incredibly, was Pixie, was a law unto herself. When the class was facing the front, she was facing the back. When the class was doing sit-ups, she was doing press-ups.

When the class was doing forward bends, she was doing back bends and crashing into the women in front and behind. Worst of all, at the end of the fifth rendering of Lily the Pink (this being the only record available), as even the most hardcore of the Beaufort woman were heaving sighs of relief at the brief respite from the assault on their ears, Pixie's ill-timed fart ripped through the hall with such ferocity that the instructor lunged for the arm of the record player and fairly threw it back onto the disc.

As Clare and Maire were returning to their car after class, Pixie waddled up.

'Helloooo Maire' she called 'and how're tings with you and Donal and the boys?'

'Fine, fine, thank you Pixie,' said Maire, 'have you met Clare from the valley, Clare this is Finbar's sister Pixie.'

'Pleased to meet you,' said Clare, 'yes we know Finbar from across the glen.'

'Ah, Finbar,' sighed Pixie, a tear welling up in her eye, 'What a…a…. kind boy. Well I'll be seeing ye again soon, don't be afraid to drop in anytime for a drop a tay.'

Once in the car Maire fairly burst with the story of Pixie. She was, according to Maire, another victim of the nerves. Over the years she'd been put on stronger and stronger doses of drugs, but now even they seemed to have lost control over Pixie's behaviour.

Maire clucked: 'The way she was carrying on in that exercise class, it's a crying shame. That woman use to cook and keep house for her husband and two boys, and now the two boys have flown the nest, the husband can't stand even to come home from the fields the food is so bad. And the shtate of the house…Spends her days wandering along the lonely farm roads around Beaufort. And don't mention Finbar, she's prone to go hysterical at the very hearing of his name.'

As Murphy's law would have it, from then on almost every time Clare passed through Beaufort she would spot Pixie walking along the road. But not before Pixie spotted her. Pixie would inevitably flag her down and pass the time of day until the pressure from a car behind would force Clare to move along.

On this day, there was no impatient car to the rescue so the conversation could have gone on unendingly. But topics were getting scarce and Clare either forgot the golden rule or simply had nothing else to say.

'So how's Finbar?' she asked.

Ciaran, then two, was strapped into his car seat. Thus far he had not participated in the conversation, but in recognition of the name which he'd heard often recently, he suddenly decided to make a contribution.

'Finbar fell in the fire,' he yelled out from the backseat.

Pixie's face contorted in misery. She let out a low wail, and took off up the country lane with her arms shaking and hands waving like Tintin's sherpas when they spotted the Yeti in Tibet.

15. TROUBLE AT THE PEARLY GATES

'Did you see that?' I called across to Clare.

It was a desperate night. The wind was howling, the car was lurching from side to side, buffetted by gusts of wind and rain. The headlights visibility was blocked by silver streaks of rain. Huge pools of water was spilling all over the road, as the ditches on either side were full to the brim. The wheels were sending cascades of water up into the wheel rims, further impeding progress and increasing the roar of the storm inside the car. My thoughts jumped to water on the spark plugs and the car petering out just as an abandoned vehicle came into view half obstructing the road. We just managed to squeeze past.

We had just past the Glencuttaun crossroads before the turning up the borreen which led to our cottage and I had caught sight of a yellow shiny apparition on the side of the road.

'Yes,' Clare shouted above the noise of the engine, wipers, demister, wind and rain.

'What was it' I asked.

'I dunno, something standing there, it looked like a mule', she said.

'It was bigger than that.'

We continued our journey up the narrow lane to our cottage. The track had been turned into a torrent of water. We made it home, soaked from having to get out and open three sets of gates.

Over the ensuing weeks and months, we would pass Glencuttaun cross and became aware of something standing there, usually in the early evening. One day we asked our neighbour Sheila about this weird phenomena.

'Oh that's Billy Mor, you know the brother of Una Mor. Haven't you met him?'

'No,' we said, 'where does he live?'

"He lives with Una and Muiris Mor, Thady and his wife and their small baby, and any one of Una's other brothers or children who pop by for a visit. And she's got some right screwballs for relatives. The one son is a practising IRA member, Gerry's his name. Haven't you seen the guards vehicles parked outside their gate whenever Gerry's around. He's supposed to have killed a few people, but they just haven't been able to nail the fecker yet. Gerry doesn't give a shite, he goads the guards in public. Una is terribly embarrassed, but the love of her family comes first, and to be honest, I think he's persuaded her a little of the rightness of his cause.'

'Who's he supposed to have killed?' I asked

'Names of people have been mentioned, but they wouldn't be known around these parts. Its just the IRA conducting their money-making in the Republic, you know they make lots of money all over the place that keeps them going - like the buildings and pubs. Especially pubs. There's always squabbles over that, battles for turf, as they say. Haven't you had a drink in that pub next to O'Grady's in Killorglin? That's a provo pub,' said Sheila warming to the subject.

'Then there's Billy.' She continued: 'The one you've seen on the side of the road. He was left a large amount of money from some relative in America, and for fifteen years he drank it. Did nothing else. It took him fifteen years to drink away the fortune. When there was nothing left, he had nowhere to go, couldn't pay rent, was absolutely useless for anything most especially because his brain had gone soft like, couldn't function at all, at all. By the way have you noticed the size of him? Six foot six, and he must be all of four hundred pounds. So when there's nowhere for him to go, Una and Muiris take him in. Billy just sleeps and occasionally gets up and eats. Then one day Una decides it's no good and Billy's not getting any better. So she orders that he must take a daily walk. She goes and buys him the gear, big wellies, a full length yellow plastic rain suit and a hat. And every night no matter what the weather, he slowly walks off up to Glencuttaun cross and stands there for an hour before walking back home. That's what you see standing there at the crossroads.'

'And by the way, maybe you should avoid Gerry, the IRA son, he might just end up thinking you're an Brit buying up land in the valley." Sheila laughed at the thought.

I was not as amused at this notion as Sheila was, in fact it disturbed me immensely. I immediately began thinking of a way of overcoming this potentially dangerous consequence to ourselves. One day when I knew Gerry the IRA man was at home, I went to the house and knocked on the door. There was a long delay before the door was swung wide open and a tall thin blond fellow, younger than I had expected was looking down his nose at me. Was I looking into the eyes of a practised killer? If I was, it didn't feel so bad. But I still wasn't going to take a chance.

'Hi' I said in my most pointed Afrikaner accent. 'I'm the South African who lives up the valley.'

'South African?' he said to me.

'Yes, have you ever been there?' I wanted to emphasize the South

African point to establish with certainty my non-English credentials.

Gerry appeared unmoved. 'No. What are you doing here?'

'Well, you know our grandparents were Irish and we came back here to where they came from.' I said.

'So how do you like the place?' I thought I detected a lightening up in his tone.

'Great! Absolutely fabulous. The people are all so friendly, and the place is beautiful.' I said gushingly, but then I couldn't resist adding, ' and such wonderful weather."

He seemed satisfied with this response. I asked him if his mother was in knowing she wasn't, and then said goodbye, considering my mission to have been accomplished, and warmed by the prospect of staying alive a little longer.

On odd occasions over the next three years we would see Billy standing like a mule at the cross. He didn't even salute the cars, all the occupants of which he knew. He just stood there, head bowed and staring at one spot. It was a pathetic sight.

Then one day Billy was dead.

The news was up and down the valley in a flash. Apparently Billy had not made an appearance long past his normal rising hour, and Una had entered his room to get him up. But Billy had fallen asleep for the last time. By the time Una tried to rouse him he was stone cold and the first signs of stiffness were beginning to set in.

Una collapsed . She was the matriarch of the house, she organised and ruled all and sundry fairly and firmly, and nobody lifted a finger without prior instruction by herself. But she fell apart on this one. As hopeless as Billy had been, Una was devoted to him completely. And now that he was dead, she couldn't think straight. As soon as she began to think about what needed to be done, the thought of Billy dead and gone overwhelmed her and she collapsed in tears and blamed herself for his death. If only she had checked on him late last night or even early this morning she might have gotten the doctor up and he would still be with us. The fact that she had never checked on him before, and that there was no good reason why she should, did not cross her distressed mind. She was suffering an acute attack of the nerves.

Normally in such circumstances, the body would have been sent down to town where the formality of establishing cause of death would be undertaken and the body prepared for return to the house, cleaned and embalmed for lasting through the wake and into the grave.

Una couldn't bring herself to organising these things on the first day, and already by the second morning, not only was the body completely stiff but beginning to whiff a little.

The family got Una to agree that it was too late to go through all the procedures, and to proceed straight to organising the wake as soon as possible. They would just get a coffin delivered up to the house and Billy could lie in state in his own room.

The coffin was delivered up to the house that same day. Not only had Billy's size been underestimated, but it was also more difficult given the stiffness, to squeeze him in. The coffin was too small. It was returned to the coffin maker who worked overtime to do something bigger. Late that night a new one had been delivered, and all the menfolk were required to give a hand in dressing, and then settling into the coffin the four hundred pound Billy. Billy had been dead for at least forty eight hours and the smell was beginning to permeate the room. As big as he was, the process of decomposition was now so advanced that he was beginning to expand.

Next morning the wake was on, and everyone from far and wide was there. Besides the fact that Una and Muiris Mor both came from huge families, they were immensely popular with the valley folk on account of their family never crossing swords with the other valley folk. This unique phenomenon, not having enemies in the valley, could only be ascribed to the fact that Muiris came from the mountains behind Lough Cloon, a spot so isolated that the community of a few families had developed a way of speaking that was totally unintelligible to anyone else. Nobody ever understood what Muiris said, consequently he could not have any enemies. A huge crowd came to offer their condolences.

The smell had now permeated the whole house, people were gagging as they went into Billy's room to offer a last prayer. The ever-expanding corpse was now wedged firmly in the coffin.

Early the following morning he was scheduled to be boxed up and driven down to the church for the last ceremony and burial.

The hearse arrived on time, and the men disappeared into the room to bring Billy out. At first six men took the coffin and edged it to the door. There was no way it could be taken out of the room horizontally as its length could not take the bend into the passage. The men were sweating, not only from the weight but also the stink could not now be tolerated without someone collapsing in a faint. A conference was held outdoors and after much deliberation it was decided to try and prise Billy from the room in the vertical position and that all parties involved would have to use handkerchiefs and cloths as masks. If this failed, the window would be demolished and Billy would depart the house that way. The second attempt to extricate Billy was then attempted.

There were now eight men, in a tiny room manhandling an immense body wedged inside a vertical coffin. At one point it was tilted too far and Billy on the open side had one of the men pinned against the cupboard before it was yanked too far the other way nearly crushing two men on that side. It was all a problem of space compounded by Una who was darting around like a fox terrier in between the struggling men, ensuring that Billy was as comfortable as possible through the terrible ordeal.

The men took it in turns to flee outside, gulping down fresh air before re-setting the masks and returning to the job at hand. It was two hours before Billy emerged through the front door flanked by eight ashen faced men who had tried to play down their discomfort so as not to hurt Una's feelings. The coffin was laid on the concrete path for the lid to be bolted on.

That task accomplished Una broke down again. She was back in a state of shock, inconsolable. The hearse disappeared off to town to put the coffin in church and the crowd returned home to wait for prayers that afternoon.

There was an equally large turnout at the Catholic church in Killorglin for the funeral service. The Killorglin church was indeed impressive. Like most other small to medium towns in Ireland it was by far the grandest, most imposing building in town. The huge cut stone structure, the arches, the volumetric space inside, the glasswork struck awe even into impartial visitors. Unlike their French, Italian or even Spanish equivalents, the Irish churches are less gaudy, but still impressive enough to help keep a flock from getting uppity.

The mourners filled in with reverential expressions, nodding sombre greetings to neighbours and relatives. A little knot of young men stood in the doorway, lighted cigarettes hidden in cupped hands. These were the rebels. Rebel enough not to sit down in a pew and pray, but not rebel enough to defy coming altogether.

Then the priest arrived in his big pointy hat, his robe glittering gold on white. The service started. The priest began chanting a well-known Latin sound track. Everyone recognised the lyrics by sound, but no one had the faintest clue what any of it meant. Just the Hail Mary's at various stopping points along the way. It went on and on, like a mantra, but without feeling, a formality that had to be got through. The priest turned the pages of his leather bound book with the gold-leafed edges one by one, while the congregants nodded and dozed and automatically joined in the Hail Mary's. The priest paused for breath, and into the sudden silence there was an almighty CRACK as loud as a full-bore shotgun with an echo that rent the church rafters. The coffin lid that had been firmly screwed down into the wood of the coffin, had, under pressure from the continued expansion of Billy actually broken the steel screws and lifted off.

It was almost as if Billy had reached the pearly gates - and what independent observer would deny that the pomp and glitter of the occasion in contrast to Billy's pointless life must have seemed as such - and that god's representative had met him for the crucial interview and found Billy wanting.

The priest and his assistants appeared unmoved by the event. Sure they watched as the resettled around the unhinged lid - they would not have been human if they hadn't - but with such nonchalance it was as if it had happened by pre-arrangement with some higher power. Of course this unholy demonstration was good for the priest's public relations with a gradually diminishing flock, because the flock was in a state of cowering terror. And who can blame them? There were gasps, there were hands lifted to mouths, there were arms raised protectively to faces with eyes peeping underneath, until it was clear that this almighty expression of wrath was over It did however serve as a warning - go to the pearly gates with a poor record at your peril. The priests happily prepared themselves for a rush of confessions in the coming days.

16. POSTMAN PADRAIG

Living in the country, one's awareness changes. A country dweller may observe the landscape and immediately pick up any inconsistency in its appearance or activity, in the same way that a city dweller might notice a sound inconsistent with the urban norm, a variable inaudible to a visitor from the country.

Over the years we had acclimatized to the silence. If a large truck or tractor drove up the road on the other side of the valley, one would instinctively look and see what was causing the slight but perceptible change in sound. Likewise when a vehicle turned up the one-kilometre track through three gates to our cottage, long before the actual noise was audible, one could feel a vibration through the earth and know that a visitor was on the way. Bizarrely, considering one of major complaints of our isolation was the lack of human contact, whenever Clare and I felt that vibration our hearts would sink.

We felt the vibe at approximately five thirty one quiet, overcast afternoon. Ten minutes later, Paudy O'Sullivan's battered yellow Ford Escort came into view. Clare and I groaned. What made matters worse, was that Paudy was alone. At least when he was accompanied by his father, Paddy, the old guy would chat away about all and sundry and hardly notice that no-one was listening, let alone contributing. But Paudy just sat, and we felt that unless we forced the pace there was absolutely no chance of proceedings moving towards an early conclusion. So we went through the whole sequence.

'How's Paddy and Brid, how's things on the farm, hasn't the weather just been desperate, I see your exhaust hanging low, have you a problem with it?' For two hours we went through the motions, tough, tough, going. Paudy looked a little agitated throughout the visit, and I began to think there must be some motive hitherto undetected for his presence. Another three quarters of an hour went by, and at 8.15pm to be exact Paudy finally blurted:

'What's the time?' He'd never worn a watch, a piece of equipment considered superfluous to someone who got up when it was light and went to bed when it was dark, seven days a week, three hundred and sixty five days a year (three hundred and sixty six if it was a leap year, but Paudy wouldn't have noticed an extra one thrown in every four years.)

'Its eight fifteen, Paudy."

'Yerrah,' he stammered, clearly trying to get something out. "Would it be okay, like, if I were to use the ah, telephone like. I've got the money right here' he said digging in his pocket and pulling out some coins.

It was out. Hallelujah. It had taken three hours but we'd got there, now we could finish up and go to bed. The darkness outside signaled that it was past his bedtime.

'Sure Paudy, please man, use the phone. No need to pay for the call unless you're phoning America,' I joked.

'No, no, I won't be doing that at all, at all. Besides, I knows no-one in America like.'

He went over to the phone and dialed a number. Some minutes later he replaced the receiver.

'No one home.' He announced.

'Why not just try again, in case you got the wrong number or something.' I suggested.

'No,' he said, 'they told me to phone before eight or they'd be out after.'

If the road vibe was somewhere in the middle of the day, it was likely to be another kind of menace all together, namely Padraig. Padraig the postman. Then we suffered mixed emotions. For while the receipt of correspondence was always welcome - even a bill served to confirm that the world still recognised us as vaguely active participants in it. But to receive the bill, one had first to receive Padraig.

Padraig the postman. What is it about post men and post women the world over? Films are made about them, they are written about in books, everyone has one in one form or another, they are a part of life as we know it, an integral, sometimes intimate part of our lives, and yet they are outside it. Ignored and forgotten where possible, in your face given half a chance. Padraig was all of these things.

A postman in rural Ireland had a particularly difficult job. Because of the fiercely private nature of the inhabitants and their activities it was imperative that the postman adopted a highly professional attitude to his work. After all, it was only the postman who knew, or could know, the real state of people's affairs. He would know the general nature of their economic activity and therefore what they might be eligible for in terms of assistance from the state. He would know if you were really disabled, if you received sheep quota monies or the dole, because he was the one delivering the forms, notices, and questionnaires. If you were receiving assistance from a rich relative overseas, if you had paying tenants, if you rented out your house or land —Padraig 'The Postie' would know. And if Padraig was invited in to a house for tea where the inhabitant was in 'dishpute' with the next door neighbor, who knows what beans might be spilt to the detriment of one or both? All of this made it imperative that The Postie conducted himself with utmost discretion.

Two other unfortunate pieces of baggage were associated with Padraig the postman. Any state job was regarded as the best a person could have. No matter what it was. A state job was a job for life, with perks that farmers working disadvantaged farmland could never dream of affording. Even clothing was supplied. A postman had to work against the envy of hard working, meagre earners.

From birth Padraig had been sickly, the runt in a particularly robust litter. The family was not only physically sturdy, but it boasted some big achievers in politics. Padraig's aunt was a TD - Member of the Dail. So a soft job was found for young Padraig. He was stiff, fragile and anemic. He moved at snail's pace. He wore his thick woolen postie jacket buttoned to the neck with what looked like a supplementary cravat to prevent any chill from sneaking close to his delicate chest. In his jacket pocket was a folded white handkerchief which he applied gently to the side of his nose, always red and slightly chapped about the opening. His hair was dirty but brushed. Obviously that delicate body was not subjected to the dangers of a bathtub all that often. His leather shoes, however, were always immaculately polished.

The valley folk didn't like being told what to do, indeed they never had. They had been warned of approaching invaders by the famous puk (goat) of Killorglin in the days of yore; they'd resisted the English before and for so long since the puk, it wasn't worth remembering. They'd died at it in the famine, and they taken up arms against the 'Tans in these very hills one generation before that which was still living. They'd lived a history of silence, and silence equaled survival. They were not about to be deprived now of any benefits to which they were entitled, or for that matter of any to which they might not be entitled, but had been cute enough to secure through the state's over zealous agent, The Postie. It was bad enough having to skirt around the dreaded customs police - the 'white squad', the Guards, the dole office, social security officers, or even the social workers and maternity nurses who visited the homes of those with new babies to check that all was well. They were all keeping an eye on that lot up the valley – and probably much else besides - but definitely that lot up the valley.

Padraig the postman was, for all these reasons, not one to be invited in, unless of course you needed to use his knowledge of all things local to get some dirt on a neighbour. Then that little green Toyota van with An Post on the side would be seen outside someone's door without its occupant, and you'd know that something was afoot. Sometimes inviting Padraig inside would simply be a scare tactic, and in this way he played the role of subterranean bogey man.

No-one could quite work out how Padraig's head was screwed on. At times his mind seemed as anemic as his body and he was able to elicit sympathy for his pathetic state as in: 'poor Padraig, Lord bless him, that boy's soft in the head'. At other times when he was fishing for dirt on someone pity would change to loathing as in: 'That nosy Padraig, lazy fecker, always looking for some shite to walk himself into'.

Some days we would hear the toot of his horn when there was a howling gale down the valley. We'd throw on some wellingtons, stick up an umbrella, and head out into the weather, because you knew that Padraig sure as hell wasn't about to get out of his little car in that, and if you wanted your post, you'd better go and get it. And so you'd be standing in a blizzard with the umbrella about to be turned inside out, and Padraig would open his van window three centimeters and pass out the letters one by one as he scrutinized each one and called out the name. You would want to grab him by the throat and pull him out the van.

'Now Tim,' he would say through the gale and the window crack, 'here's one from South Africa - oh, now that's a long way away isn't it?' Once, when he dropped his vigilance and his window more than the usual slit, I leaned through, grabbed the letters and ran inside. On a good weather day, Padraig would roll down the window and turn off the engine. 'Now what's happening to that old stone cottage on Timmy-John's farm next door? I heard it was sold to some English people.'

'I don't know,' I lied

'Well I can tell you now there's something going on with that house right next door to your own, and I bet Timmy-John got a tidy little sum from someone or other. Nice easy money made,' Padraig rambled on, watching me carefully. He would say things and watch for a reaction. He did not require words. The involuntary reaction - the body language, the squirm and the shuffle was answer enough for him.

At times, I would tell him things that were not true just for sport, but he never took the bait.

'Well that's not what I heard,' he would say accusingly. He would then repeat what he had heard and watch for the reaction.

That was Padraig, Padraig the postman. Creep.

Given the nature of Padraig and his habits, it is only natural that he should have provided the root cause of the breakdown that would lead to our giving up our life in Ireland. Of course it would not be by design, it would just be one of those unfortunate actions or omissions of his, the ramifications of which he would be too disinterested to think through.

Whichever way we were to look at our existence in Ireland, Sheila held the key. Socially, we were surviving with respect to the people in the valley. We had been unable to do any better in the town, besides it was a little too far for contact to be anything other than formal. We'd been pretty much unable to build any solid friendships around things in common, so it was Sheila who provided that bit of interaction which prevented total isolation. It was an isolation which even I was forced to admit was not particularly attractive, especially with children who would, as the years went by, be more and more demanding of company other than Clare's and mine.

Biddy Boon had introduced us to Sheila prior to our move from Lakeview house into our own cottage at Dromleagh. We'd been to her stations, popped in for the odd cup of tea, and Sheila's daughter Sera, under her mother's guidance had become Ciaran's regular baby-sitter. Sera, then fifteen, had become indispensible. Every Saturday afternoon, Sera minded Ciaran in their home, giving Clare a welcome break. Through this interaction, and the fact that we were close neighbours (in country terms), a solid bond had formed between us, and Clare would often stop by Sheila's house for a cup of tea before making her way back home.

Sheila was our nearest neighbour. As you turned off the road onto the boreen which led to our house, there were two pieces of land to traverse before getting to the Mullane's on whose land our cottage was sited. The first gate opened onto Sheila's land, a second gate enclosed her land and opened onto that of Timmy-John Sullivan before the third gate leading to our cottage. This meant that a potential visitor to our home had to contemplate the opening and closing of three farm gates. Without diligently closing the gates the animals, either sheep or cattle, would stray onto the next door farm, and all hell would break loose. The straying of animals was probably the cause of more battles between neighbours than anything else. The scarcity of decent grazing land meant every lush blade of grass was protected with fury and fist.

The gates were the bane of our lives. If we took a trip to Killorglin to buy a loaf of bread, it was three gates to open and close just to get out. If you were alone, this meant hopping out of the car a total of twelve times, most often in a roaring gale with bullets of rain driving down one's neck. Those gates were to be the final nails in the coffin of our Irish idyll.

Sheila kept a small herd of cattle that would deliver up milk every day and three or four calves per year for the market. It was hard work tending to the animals, and the land on which they depended. But Sheila loved her animals, and when each of the calves grew into heifers and was dispatched to market, she would cry real tears, tears that were never squeezed out of her for anything else. The income from the sale of the cows combined with her husband Seamus' meagre income from working shifts washing dishes in the hotels in Killarney was just sufficient to pay the monthly bills.

To help her with the gathering of cows and also for company Sheila kept a few dogs. Her favourite was a sandy coloured sheep dog called Jack. Jack was indeed special. Besides being highly intelligent and good natured he was astonishing looking, for one of his eyes was bright light blue and the other was so dark brown it looked black. So depending on which side of the face one looked at the dog seemed to have two personalities. Ciaran spent much of his Saturdays at Sheila playing with Jack.

Sheila's husband Seamus worked whatever shifts he could find. If he finished one shift here, he fitted another in there, and so on and so forth, until as many days and nights as he could find in a week, in a month, in a year, were packed with dish washing. At whatever time he returned home there was scarcely time for a hang sandwich, which was served to him like a dog away from the rest of the family. Awaiting him were so many tasks and chores as two men could not fit in. Cut and split logs, attend to the turf, repair fences, repair the house, the cow sheds, the water supply, the car, lift the kids. Seamus worked like a pack horse. He even looked a bit like a pack horse, being squat with a dark mop of hair and huge bags under darting, hunted eyes. He never openly questioned his lot in life. Life was not about trying to find an easy way. There was no easy way. Life was tough. It was about work, if you could find it. Once you found it, you grasped it like a lion grasped its prey.

In a rare moment of recreation for Seamus, he and I went together to a crucial All Ireland Gaelic football semi final clash between Kerry and Cork in Killarney.

And then twice as fast as it had taken our relationship to develop to this state of mutual benefit and co-operation, it all fell apart.

Sera was increasingly unavailable for the Saturday afternoon with Ciaran and Sheila was mysteriously not at home when Clare showed up for an impromptu visit - even though all the signs were there that someone had hurriedly vacated the house and taken to the forest of holly trees at the back of the house. Clare and I debated whether these incidents were simply a series of unfortunate near misses, or were we being frozen out? If the latter were true, we racked our brains to think of reasons why.

Then the most obvious incidence of avoidance happened. Clare and I were returning from town after shopping at eleven am one morning and had passed through the first gate, and had arrived at the second. As Clare was driving, I hopped out of the car and opened the gate. There was a rustling of the undergrowth and Jack, Sheila's dog, emerged barking excitedly, his tail wagging. I petted Jack and looked up for Sheila, for the two of them were inseparable. But Sheila was nowhere to be seen. At first I was puzzled and shouted out her name a couple of times. Then the penny dropped: she was hiding in the bushes. We went on our way. I was furious at this immature display and Clare was devastated. At least the cards were on the table.

Clare was determined to confront Sheila, which she did some days later when she finally trapped Sheila at home. Unable to control her emotions, Clare burst into tears, demanding of Sheila what difficulty she had with us, what had we done or not done that Sheila found it necessary to hide away in the bushes when we passed by. At first Sheila said she never saw or heard us and that there was no problem, but Clare was in such a state that Sheila became concerned. She'd never seen such a display of naked soul baring, except of course in the pub at the end of an evening when sufficient alcohol had loosened the faculties, but that was normal and never to be taken seriously. Here was someone sober and sobbing at eleven o'clock in the morning.

'Well why don't you people close the fecking gates,' she finally blurted out.

The flood of Clare's tears stopped as if by the dropping of a sluice gate. At last she had something. For a moment she was stunned.

'What gates?' she asked, momentarily unable to comprehend what Sheila was talking about.

'Those gates in my field. Everyday I'm running all over Timmy-John's land looking for my cows, and then chasing his blashted sheep off my own land.'

'But we close those gates everytime, come rain or storm, I swear to it - even though half the time they are nearly broken off and I have to break my back dragging them across the road, with a baby screaming its head off in the car.

Clare tried to muster a semblance of reason as anger replaced confusion: 'Anyway, why didn't you tell me about it, I was here every damned second day having tea with you, why couldn't you just say something to me.'

'Its not for me to tell you what to do or what not to do. So help me God, you make your own decisions, girl. But remember this, you may come and go but we've been here a long time and aren't going anywhere.'

On this ominous note, Clare left in a state of shock. She knew that our relationship with Sheila was over, and our continued stay in Ireland would be just that much less pleasant as a result. We'd taken a massive step into that landscape, that pastoral landscape in which everybody hates one another. Where neighbours jostle and connive against each another, revelling in the misfortune, the downfall, the ruin, of one of their number. And yet, in times of crisis, or under threat, real or imagined, they are forced together in communal support in order to survive.

By the time she got home Clare's vulnerable emotions had hardened into steely resolve. We undertook an immediate post mortem. It was true that we had never knowingly or deliberately left the gates open. Of course the gate could have been left open through absent mindedness, but this would have been very rare. Logically working through all the possibilities and permutations, we came to the same conclusion. There could only be one culprit, one person responsible for the events that led had led to this social destruction - Padraig the postman. Padraig with his delicate constitution, Padraig with his frail and anemic body under that postie jacket and cravat, could not be bothered to pull his body out of that little An Post van and close the gates.

I relished my confrontation with him on this matter, although I already knew it would serve no meaningful purpose. The damage was done, and no amount of explaining, no number of apologies nor promises, would rescue our relationship with Sheila's family. 'Padraig, could you please make doubly sure that you close the gates on the way out, because the animals are moving through and people are blaming us,' I said in what I thought was a neutral tone to Padraig.

'Now you would obviously be thinking that it is me responsible for leaving gates open,' he replied defensively.

'I don't care who it might or might not have been,' I said, 'I'm just requesting that we be very careful about this in the future.'

Padraig wasn't having it: 'Anyways, I'm not sure it's part of my job description to open so many fucking gates. I'm supposed to deliver letters, not keep animals in the right place.'

'Well, I will put a postbox on the main road and you can post them there without coming up here."

'It's against regulations,' he smarmed. ' I have to deliver post onto the property of the receiver or into their hand. So unless you buy that field down there, or you come down and fetch the post, we carry on as we are. And believe me that makes me sadder than you, cause it's me that must open and close them fucking gates.'

And with that he withdrew his scrawny neck and dripping nose from the window frame and fired up the van, joggling back down the lane, in a pompous puff of winner's superiority.

17. A MOUNTAIN TOO FAR

Much like the prison system there were several categories of blow-in. Category A comprised non-English speakers, Germans, French, Dutch and Japanese, although the Japanese were out on such a limb they might just as well have been polar bears. Category A inmates spoke with funny accents and used funny words. After spending much time in Ireland, the English they spoke was with an Irish accent, so not only were the words funny, but they were pronounced with an Irish-French or Irish-German accent. A highlight was to hear them use favoured local expressions like feck, fuck, cunt, hoor, eedjit, cratur, shite and craic: Category A folk didn't always know what those words meant, but they knew from careful mimicry of the Irish, just where they went in a sentence.

Within category A there were two sub-categories, those who lived in Ireland permanently, and those who just had a holiday home. Besides the language difficulty the category A1 blow-in inevitably suffered another affliction: they were often Jehovah's Witnesses. The year 2 000 was a biggie for Jehovah's Witness, because they were all supposed to die. Our story unfolded in the last decade of the previous millennium, so the idea that the world was about to end, tended to affect one's ability to establish long term relationships with them. If you were like us, desperately looking for friends, you could forget it with category A1.

Category B were the English speakers with Irish connections. There are zillions of people all over the world with solid Irish credentials. First, second, third, fourth generation Irish emigrants some who have done incredibly well all over the outside world. Some have ruled countries, like the Kennedys in America, some have populated whole continents like Australia, and some have reached the pinnacle of success in fields as diverse as sport and art. One can just as easily run into a successful Irishman in Botswana or Burundi (and I have) as one can in Bahrain or Bermuda. But when they return to Ireland they're just another 'fecking blow-in'.

Category C folk were, in a sense, the least fortunate of all. For they were born in Ireland, they lived in Ireland, their families were born and lived in Ireland, their families on both sides before that were born and lived in Ireland. Quite possible, not a single errant relative had ever emigrated from Ireland in ten generations. All members of all the families had been receiving one state subsidy or another since the beginning of state subsidies. That's how Irish they were. But they were still blow-ins. Why? Because they had moved to, or got married into, a family in the next valley. This was explained to me by a woman who had married into a family in our valley. She came from Beaufort. Although it was in the same magisterial district and a distance of some seven miles, it was a mountain too far and she was a blow in with all the diminished human rights that status entailed. If the valley folk were discussing the disgrace of Ned The Banker Liddy living with his niece and the Beaufort woman ventured an opinion, she would be instantly cut out by the party with a curt: 'Shut-up Vera, you don't even know the family.'

But these are merely broad blow-in brushstrokes. It is necessary to illustrate these definitions with live humans.

Otto Bauhaus was a category A2 blow-in. A German who had bought a holiday cottage at first, and later a piece of land for which he claimed the state forestry grant, and had planted with deciduous trees. Otto understood perfectly how to get by happily and unmolested as a despised foreigner and what were the best methods of property preservation. It was a simple formula and it worked like a dream: pay people. He paid someone to keep an eye on his house, he paid someone to look after his car, he paid someone for a load of logs or turf, whenever Otto was around there was little bits of cash for this and that. While he always paid people, he never bought anything in Ireland.

The reason why Otto wouldn't buy anything in Ireland was that according to him everything in Ireland was rubbish. Otto was a technically minded guy, and if a techno-boffin is a scary thing, a German techno-boffin defies speech. Otto's demands for specification excellence and exemplary workmanship, meant that nothing in Ireland could possibly be worth purchasing. When the family came for their month long summer holiday, and then again their two weeks holiday at Christmas, it was usually in their Toyota Land Cruiser with a trailer holding everything required to sustain themselves for the period. Including German sausage. Of course, this aspect of them added to the locals' complete non-comprehension of the blow-in category A2.

When the Bauhaus' decided to rebuild the old stone cottage ruin on the land they bought for the forestry, they had to bring the building materials from Germany. It was not possible to bring only some of the materials because the Irish had got wise to unscrupulous scams. The importation of cheaper foreign plumbing pipes could make someone a nice little turn in Ireland. The Irish state then employed many devious tricks to stop such activity. For example, in the case of the plumbing pipes on the plumbing pipes, the Irish version was of a slightly smaller bore than that on the continent. So if you were building your house and ran out of pipe and went to the local hardware and bought some more only to find that they were the wrong size and you were stuck until your next trip to England, France or Germany. Otto admired greatly this piece of technical guile by the Irish, but still not enough to buy anything locally.

To rebuild his house therefore, he had to bring the whole shebang (short of the rocks) from Germany. He procured the largest trailer that his three and a half litre top of the range Toyota Land Cruiser could tow, and stashed everything needed to build a house inside it. At a top speed of sixty kilometers per hour, he drove his groaning cargo across Germany and Holland, onto the Channel ferry to England. Irritated by the need to change currency at these regular intervals, Otto decided not to bother. *Besides he'd always supported the notion of a single European currency.* While driving along he had many hours to contemplate how to overcome the problem of the need to purchase things like petrol (which was not brought from Germany) without the proper currency. In Derby, England, he pulled into a garage.

Otto alighted from his Land Cruiser, removed the cap from the petrol tank and filled his very thirsty vehicle to the brim. He replaced the cap and proceeded to the cashier who had already rung up the huge amount on a computerised till. He placed a wad of German marks on the counter and looked the cashier straight in the eye.

'What's that?' she asked.

'Money,' Otto replied.

'We can't take that.'

'O,' he said, ' is it for free?'

'No it's not free, but that's not English money.'

She looked at him in that contemptuous way English people look at foreigners, though not quite sure what she was dealing with. Was he a crazy? Was he a crook? Was he German? She was scared that he could be a combination.

'O, I'm sorry' Otto said, ready to unleash his second prepared line. 'Now, how can we separate your petrol from mine?'

She ignored him. She slipped off her high stool and picked up a nearby *Sun* newspaper. She flicked through to the financial page and looked up the exchange rate, English pounds for German marks. She scrutinised his notes and counted them. She fiddled on the calculator. She looked up at him with disgust as she dropped the notes into the till.

'No change?' Otto asked, a little smile playing in the corner of his mouth.

Now she looked him straight in the eye.

'No change,' she said through clenched teeth.

Thus they continued across England and into Wales, then on the ferry again and across the Irish channel, landing at Dun Laoghaire. Otto drove his family and cargo off the ferry and took the 'nothing to declare' exit. An Irish customs official stepped into the road and signaled them to pull over.

The customs man stuck his head in the window and demanded: 'What have you got in the trailer?'

The Bauhaus's had by now been on the road for more than forty eight hours, and the last thing Otto felt like was an EU-approved diplomatic conversation.

'My house,' he said, without an ounce of humour.

The customs man could play that game. 'Your house, eh? Very nice to have your house right here with you, I'm sure. Would you mind pulling into that warehouse over there and showing me your house please sir.'

Otto pulled into the warehouse and told his wife Ulrike and son Karl-Heinz to wrap up nice and cosy in the sleeping bags in the Land Cruiser. It was going to be a long night.

Otto got out of the vehicle. The customs man joined him next to the trailer, and looking in his passport said,

'Now Mr....eh..Bauhaus, you say you have your house in the trailer.'

'Ja, I haf,' said Otto.

'May I see it, please?'

Otto opened the side awning to reveal doors and frames, windows and glass, pipes, toilet, bath, basin, packs of tongue in groove boarding, boxes and boxes of tools and equipment, steel sheeting, rolls of fibre insulation, paint ... pretty much everything in fact needed to build a house.

'Now how can I be knowing that this material is not for sale in Ireland, and that you're not just taking it in to pay for your holidays.'

'Because I'm telling you zis is my house, and if I tell you zis is my house, zis is my house,'

'Perhaps you'd like to prove that to me, Mr......eh....Bauhaus,' said the smart customs man.

'If you command me to do so, I vill do so.' said Otto.

The customs man smirked: 'I command you to do so.'

Hearing these words, Ulrike and Karl-Heinz snuggled deeper into their bags and prepared to sleep. Otto pulled some papers from his briefcase and laid them on the concrete floor. They were the plans of his house. Removing his leather jacket, he donned overall and gloves and started unpacking the trailer.

Two hours later, Otto had the door frames in position, with the doors, locks, hinges and screw sets laid out. The window frames were going up, the packs of glass were lying in the correct position alongside the correct frames with enough putty in a pack for each. Otto was busy on the roof, sorting out which sheets went where and lining-up the ridge capping.

The customs man had long since disappeared into the office and had been standing looking out on this scene with a cup of coffee in his hand pointing out to all the other customs men who were grinning and laughing at this German eedjit working away on his house.

Midnight came around, marking the end of the customs man's shift. He emerged from the office and addressed Otto:

'Thank you, Mr....eh...Bauhaus. I think I can see it's your house. Please pack up and you can go on your way.'

'No, no,' said Otto not looking up from his work, ' you command me to unpack my house, zat is what I do.'

The customs man shuffled around for a few minutes not knowing quite what to do, eventually disappearing back into the office where all his mates had left for home. With no more ferries expected for the night, only a skeleton staff were now on hand. There was no more smiling and laughing in the office. Clearly, no one on the new shift was going to assume responsibility for the German madmen putting his house together on the forecourt. The custom's man had to see it through.

He re-emerged from the office and went over to Otto.

'Mr.....eh...Bauhaus,' he said, 'I command you to pack up and leave.'

'I cannot do zat,' said Uli.

'Why not?'

'Because I haf not completed your first command,' Otto said.

Now the custom's man lost it: 'Don't get funny with me, you fucking smartass. I'll get the guards down here now and they'll throw you back in the Irish sea so quick you won't know whether you're achtung or smachtung.'

Otto still did not look up from his work: 'Bring ze guards, and I vill have some craic wiz them as I haf wiz you. Neizer you nor ze fecking guards scare me at all, at all.'

The customs man went back into the office. It was three in the morning before Otto put the last of the plumbing joints together. He hailed the customs man who returned to inspect the house. Otto took him through every detail of it, the customs man walking behind him like a German shepherd behind its master.

At the end of the tour the customs man said:

'Thank you Mr.Bauhaus, please put your house away now and leave.'

And zat is what he did, leaving customs at six in the morning just as the customs man's third shift in a row was about to start.

Richie and Donna were category B blow-ins, that is returned English speakers of Irish descent. Richie Savage's parents had moved to the east-end of London when he was a child. Richie had spent his youth doing the markets, Brick Lane, West Ham, first as an assistant on a fruit and veg stall, graduating to sales, attracting the customers with wide boy verbals and his sense of humour. He could see himself stuck forever in the big, dirty city, and Richie wanted something better. But he didn't know any other way of life. He had married Donna, his childhood sweet heart, who was as east end tough as they come. His parents had moved back to the family plot just outside Killorglin and at the age of twenty one he and Donna followed them.

Richie immediately noticed a gap in the market: in Killorglin there was no fresh fruit and veg. Sure there were some idiots on a street corner selling cabbages, spuds and turnips, and sure there were carrots wrapped in drab plastic in the supermarket, but there was certainly no inviting, colorful stall where customers could broaden their horizons in the fresh food department of their lives. Not only did Richie believe he could persuade people with his gab to become that little bit more adventurous, he also knew the market, the prices and where to get the stuff. He was ambitious.

Richie had made a trailer that could be opened on both sides and he noticed that everyone who came to town used the car park behind the shops on the main road. He had a word with the local council who informally gave him permission to operate on that spot. And so he set up the stall in the corner of the car park and away he went. The immediate response was small town curiosity - everybody went to see his stall. Not only was it more attractive with a bigger range of good quality produce, but it was cheaper than the supermarket and the other stall. The middle classes (who never show loyalty to anything, let alone a supermarket or the local man) led the way, bringing their custom. And Richie never filled your bag with rotten stuff at the bottom and the good stuff at the top like the local man had a tendency to do. If ever you were to complain to the local man you were told in no uncertain terms to 'fook-orf, go buy your shpuds in England if you don't like our Irish ones'.

Within weeks Richie and his stall were cleaning up, so much so that he handed over the reins to a Killorglin lad, a distant family member, while Donna kept an eye on things. Richie had more important things to do. Having secured his sources of supply and established his prices, he now took to the road to market his wares round the local hotels. The chefs were as impressed by his show as the people of Killorglin and soon his van was full of produce for delivery. Without Richie on the stall there were some minor snags. One day a local woman asked the young lad on the stall what an aubergine was and how one should eat it. 'Tis the simplest ting in the world now, you just cut it up and throw it in the shalad.' There was almost a serious incident the following day when the woman returned believing that either the aubergine was rotten or had been deliberately poisoned.

But the chill Irish wind that blew under the awning of Richie's on a daily basis was about to erupt into a full blown gale. Being a street wise kid from London's toughest neighbourhood, Richie saw it coming: indeed, before he'd set foot in Ireland, he'd already written it down in the 'cons' column. He was ready.

It started with words, harsh words from the lumpens selling (in ever decreasing numbers) shpuds and turnips on the street corner. But verbal abuse soon turned to threats, and then the threats became action. One night Richie's little assistant was beaten up in a pub with the words 'don't let us see you on that stall in the morning' ringing in his ears. Richie himself went back to the stall, drafting in another member of the family to drive the van and do the hotel run. Next there was a confrontation on the stall itself. Richie was heavily outnumbered and the stall was all but demolished, tomatoes squashed into the tarmac along with the blood drawn from Richie's face as he tried to defend his patch. But the next day he was back. Fresh produce on the stall, face swollen and bruised, cheerfully greeting his customers. The town was split, not so much for or against Richie but rather for Richie or for the horrible lumpens who had been unpleasant to everybody for years. No-one except other nutter blow-ins like myself, actually offered him physical support (an offer he never took up). But the shoppers at his stall gave him enough encouragement to carry on by continuing to buy from him.

Physical intimidation having failed, the lumpens opted for a subtler form of sabotage. Bringing their awning from the street corner in town, they set up shop right next to Richie in the car park. The council turned a blind eye and the guards were all of a sudden busy elsewhere. But the lumpens did even less business than they had on their street corner. Richie stood his ground: his stall remained open all hours of the day and even into the dark, long after the lumpens had retired to the pub to discuss their strategy for the next day. The stall was demolished again and again Richie fought them alone. Now Richie had started a jibe of his own: 'You're fucking soft, you have to kill me, but you can't, you're too fucking soft, you're a bunch of poofy girls,' he would say when he saw them on the street.

'Soft poofy girls, soft poofy girls, can't hurt me, can't hurt me.' He would goad them and goad them – and then take another beating. In the end Richie was right: they couldn't hurt him enough for him to leave.

Now nobody was buying from either stall. It was just too uncomfortable for anyone to go near that corner of the car park. Violence could break out any time. But Richie could afford to keep setting up because his van was also now servicing the hotels in Killarney as well as Killorglin. The lumpens couldn't survive the loss of income, so they set their stall back up in town and left him alone. Richie had won, and with his hard-earned gains he built a house on Sunhill, Killorglin's premier location, in time to welcome his and Donna's first child.

****

When Johan Vermeulen and I first met, it seemed as if it was fated to be. Twenty years earlier I had lived in a van, and each evening I would drive out of the city and park/camp in the remote countryside. Of course it was a very lonely existence because not only did I never see anybody, but before the advent of cell phones, I was totally cut off from contact with other human beings. I had a belief that if I happened to be walking about on my remote patch, and someone came walking the other way and our paths intersected, it would necessarily be true romance for all time. The logic was that the other person would be exactly the same as me. It didn't happened then, but that is what it felt like when I met Johan. There are always subtle differences between theory and reality.

We met at the motor mechanic's garage on the banks of the Laune river and next to the ruin of an old stone castle. I remember going home that night and excitedly telling Clare that finally we might have found people we'd have something in common with. I had given Johan our address and invited them up to our house on the following Sunday afternoon. Johan, his wife Lottie and their three children were Dutch, and they all had white straw-coloured Dutch hair except for Lottie who had white straw-coloured Dutch hair that came straight out of a bottle. Lottie was a designer, with a style and flair that bottomed out in short skirts and high-heeled cowgirl boots. Quite unlike the denims and wellingtons we were used to. It was very refreshing. We had everything in common, starting with the lonely blues of a category A1 blow-in.

Over the weeks and months that followed, we found out quite a lot about each other. The first startling discovery was that they were Jehovah's Witness – and very staunch members of the community at that. But they never mentioned it to us. Clare and I pondered this often. We concluded that they knew that if they witnessed Jehovah in front of us, our friendship would die as instantaneously as it had grown, and they didn't want that.

On another Sunday afternoon several weeks after our first tea with Johan and Lottie, we were travelling to our favourite Sunday spot, Glenbeigh, for a walk on the beach at Inch. To get there we always drove through the woods edging Lake Caragh, and in those trees nestled some very picturesque houses. Today as we drove through, we noticed the rear end of a large Volvo, partially obstructing the road. How is it that a make of car becomes synonymous with a certain human activity? In our neck of the woods, the only people who drove large Volvos were Jehovah's Witnesses. Everybody knew that. It could only have been that the extra protection in the side panels for which those Volvo's were famous meant that the disciples would definitely make it to the end of the millennium. Anyhow, there was the Volvo, and close by, there were the witnesses. The whole Dutch contingent led by Johan and Lottie Vermeulen supplemented by a clutch of other obvious-looking foreigners including, incredibly, what appeared to be a black person. We were intrigued at the possibility of a black blow-in persuading an Irish Catholic in those backwoods to another religion on a Sunday. Talk about a hiding to nothing.

There was another aspect to Johan that became of interest to me. I wasn't making a comfortable living. He was. He had set up a business unblocking the sewers of all the small towns in the vicinity with a big high pressure water machine mounted on the back of a truck, and there seemed to be more blocked shit than he could possibly deal with. The more he spoke about the scale of the shit he had to deal with, and at times was being overwhelmed by, the more I began thinking my future also lay in shit. He would be needing an assistant, and soon.

Whenever the discussion got onto work, we would speak about his need to grow capacity, both man and machine. Twice he invited me out on shit unblocking expeditions, to get a feel for the profession. Unlike my lambing experience and the promise that I would be a qualified vet before the night was out, dealing with blocked shit was in another league. It required certain training, and a very specific type of constitution. For example, if one anticipated being out for the day, one had to be very circumspect about the kind of breakfast one ate before boarding the truck. Even Johan confessed he didn't like the smell. Although I thought I had performed reasonably well, I saw Johan out on the road some weeks later with someone else on the truck with him. My heart fell. I felt a failure: I'd even passed my sell-by date in the world of shit. Clearly it was time to move on.

About a year after leaving Ireland, and having settled comfortably in South Africa, an envelope arrived in the post. It was from Ireland. Both Clare and I were excited; after all, very few of our Irish acquaintances were the letter-writing type. With fingers all a-tremble we ripped open the letter and out slipped a single sheet of typed written paper. This is what it read:

THIS IS A PRETTY PANTIES EXCHANGE

That's right, a pretty panties exchange.

I know it all sounds a little bit strange but please read on.

Send a new pair of panties to the first person below and send a copy of this letter to six of your friends. Move my name to 1) and put your name second, remember to mention your size.

This is not a chain letter, it's for fun. If you cannot do this within 7 days, please let men (sic) know as it's not fair on those who participate.

Send the panties in a manila envelope and hopefully the post office will take care of them and they'll arrive save and sound. If you do this you will receive 36 pairs of new panties. It is fun to see where they come from and the variety you'll get.

Remember, 36 pairs for the price of one. I challenge you to find a better bargain!!

Lottie Vermeulen.

18. BACK TO AFRICA: A LETTER TO MATTHEW

15th May 1994.

Dear Matthew,

What a joy it was to return home today to see an envelope with Eugene, USA on it, and a letter inside as well! I have so much to reply to and reflect on that I hardly know where to begin.

A shock to begin with. We are leaving Ireland permanently and returning to live in South Africa in a few weeks time. We went to Johannesburg at the end of February for the obligatory five-year family pilgrimage, and found ourselves mightily impressed by the transformation occasioned by the political change there. Though we have been contemplating a move away from Ireland for quite some time, we never thought it would be to return to South Africa after a 20-year absence.

The reasons for our wanting to leave are numerous. To go into detail would entail writing a book. This letter will attempt to describe a few.

The rain has pissed down, nay bucketed down, nay torrented down, for four straight years. This might sound like an exaggeration but I read a statistic recently that Ireland has been getting about eight feet of rain per year. That's one inch every four days. Last year we went to the beach. Once. Consequently the kids are indoor kids, the same as if we'd been living in a terraced row in London.

Every day, Ciaran (who is now four) and I would take a hike through the hills behind our cottage, irrespective of the weather. As a toddler he became obsessed with catching a baby puk (wild goat), and on most days we would spot them on the high rocks in the distance and he would go after them until I finally physically restrained him, knowing it was a long way back. But now he can't be bothered with the wellington's, the thick padding, the rain suit over top and bottom, the hat and the gloves it requires to venture into the cold rain and howling wind. He'd rather sit in front of the fire and watch cartoons on TV.

Even the locals here secretly admit that over the last few years the weather's been diabolical. I say secretly because people here take a foreigner's criticism of the weather personally.

Local lives are so small and hard that the weather assumes central importance. The preferred method of communication is through 'weather speak'. One has to gauge another's mood and willingness to converse by the adjectives used to describe the day. 'Dirty old day' means 'I'm not stopping to speak', whereas 'desperate isn't it?' is an invitation to further interaction. After four years I could never claim to know all the subtleties and meanings, but then I don't really want to. Suffice it to say even academics are busy writing papers with titles like 'the weather, the Irish and depression'.

A German friend living in the nearby town buys his newspaper at the same stand every morning on his way to work. If it's pissing down and my friend remarks to the vendor 'raining again', the paper man will say 'at least it's not cold' or 'at least it's not windy'. If there's a howling, freezing gale the paper man will say 'at least it's not frosty'. Now if the day is cold, frosty, windy, howling, wet, stormy and blustery what does yer man say? 'At least it's not dusty.' Fucking dusty, I ask you. There's no such word in the

Irish dictionary, yet it remains a last-ditch defense against criticism of the Irish weather.

So it's the people as well. When one first arrives in a new place all the differences between oneself and the locals seem interesting. You're on a voyage of discovery about them, about yourself. After all, most people here have never traveled beyond this valley and we've stayed in a few odd spots on the planet, and holidayed in a few more, so there are bound to be intriguing differences. After four years we have, by and large, established what they are. We're not likely to become sheep farmers or convert to Catholicism or have as our principle interest in life the shortcomings and goings of the neighbors. They're not likely to start listening to the Red Hot Chili Peppers, take up art, have an interest in world news or learn to eat Kiwi fruits - if such things were available. So there we are. When interest turns to boredom, what does one do? Go for a pint of Guinness, my German friend says. And if that doesn't do the trick, make it twenty pints.

So you couldn't get on with the locals, I hear you think. What about how they got on with us? The overwhelming attitude was ambivalence. Not so towards each other. Suspicion is probably the most endearing emotion people who've lived side by side for centuries feel for each other. Hatred is more common, arising most often between families over land inheritance, and between neighbors over boundaries and animals. There was a case recently of a decades old squabble between two farmers over a certain boundary, with their respective animals regularly found to be enjoying a free lunch on the other's land. There had been several instances of fisticuffs and assault charges laid. But the guards could never find any witnesses, just the two old farts slugging it out on a mountain over a piece of scraggy land and bit of wire. Then one of them was dead. Found in a ditch on the side of the road, having been hit by a car in the dead of night, walking back from the pub.

If the day ever comes that I attempt to write about the experience of living here, I know that I will not be able to include the most eccentric people and families in the valley because it would be so outlandish no-one would believe it. For example, it is common in these parts for people to make a virtue out of not finding a need for material goods or modern conveniences (like a toilet or electricity). It is also common for people to suffer various mental afflictions such as depression or schizophrenia, although names are not assigned to these maladies. But there is a family of three brothers that live in this valley, that have managed to combined these two qualities in extreme helpings. Two of whom have not been seen outside of their tiny home for twenty five years. Are they there, are they dead? No-one knows. The third brother walks to town to collect the dole by a roundabout route thereby avoiding the roads and any farmer he might perchance meet in a field, he tends some potatoes, he milks a cow and cuts some turf......and that is it. The other locals let them be unnoticed, forgotten. There is not even a story one can tell. Three men in a room for ever. Waiting for Godot. Real people are infinitely more bizarre than any fictional character – especially round these parts.

A backwoods farmer, who went by the rhythmic title of Mallachy Mulcahy and who lived not far from here, was recently driving his sheep between two bits of his own land, separated by a mountain owned by someone else.

This was accomplished most expeditiously by road as an outcrop of rock on the mountain was too treacherous to herd sheep safely across. While the farmer and his dogs were badgering the sheep up the winding road, a number of cars began to accumulate behind the flock, mostly tourists who were quite enjoying this authentic rustic spectacle. Mallachy wasn't feeling nearly so pastoral. His stress levels were zooming, each turn of his body revealing a new car in the lengthening queue.

He feverishly began yelling at his dogs, who were nipping the back legs of the last sheep, but the bulk of the numbers up ahead would not be moved any faster. He took to assisting the dogs by beating the rumps of the unfortunates at the rear, who were mounting the backs of the sheep ahead still without any noticeable progress. The farmer was now yelling and charging up and down the back ranks, little bubbles of foam escaping the corners of his mouth. His big face and bald head had turned red, his temples pulsed and bulged and hot sweat ran down his collar. The sudden pain in his chest was like a knife-stab to the heart and his temple seemed to burst. He fell to the ground and was dead in three minutes. The farmer's heart had exploded from the stress of the situation.

In my childhood and youth I came to realise that the world was sick: living in apartheid South Africa in the sixties and seventies, it wasn't hard to notice. My rebellion in early adulthood was a three-quarter hearted effort to change this state of affairs and I spent many years in pursuit of change. My efforts were ineffective. Eventually I opted to escape the horrors altogether, to seek out a clean, harmless little spot in which I could live happily ever after. By consuming little and being nice I would be doing no harm to anyone and would be rewarded with a shower of happiness. This, I've realized, is a quasi-religious viewpoint (perhaps without the quasi). There is no-one out there measuring one's performance and doling out Brownie points to the deserving. I've always thought of myself as a realist. But the notion of escape is a naive one in an increasingly global world. There is no dear, sweet valley peopled with jolly country folk, deservedly free of worry and stress.

I can take you to an absolutely magnificent spot on the cusp of the plateau looking west over Lough Acoose and the undulating hills of Glencar and beyond. The backdrop to the lake is the dramatic mountains rising steeply to the highest peak in Ireland, Carrountoohil. Then look north-east. We're standing on boggy land, close to a spring that surfaces here and burbles into a river spreading down the valley and out across distant plains towards the Slieve Mish mountains. Someone once visited us up here and remarked that it felt like the end of the world.

What they didn't know was that the remains of a hundred car wrecks were buried right here, under our feet. The Casey's earthmoving equipment dug a deep hole in the bog and the cars that Eoin and Tommy Boon tinkered with for all those years were dumped in the bottom. For a hundred years to come the gear-box oil, grease and rust will seep into the bog and flow down that pristine stream. And some future stroller will walk up that valley and kneel by the stream and take a draught of pure, crystal water and wonder why there's a tiny opaque rainbow on the surface.

Yes, it has become impossible to enjoy the environment. Dead animals litter the countryside; septic tanks spew untreated waste into pristine rivers; all manner of chemicals cover the earth to kill unwanted plant species and make the grass grow. Overgrazing rips away topsoil revealing unyielding granite; rivers and lakes die from fine filament fishing; the sea bed is hoovered clean; trees are cut down for being 'untidy'.

A year ago a young guy came up the road which ends in a cul-de-sac a kilometer on from our cottage. He drove to the end got out of his car and retrieved a chain saw from the boot. He struggled ten metres down a steep slope until he stood before the largest silver birch in the valley, its girth measuring eight feet. Then he took up his saw and felled the giant tree in fifteen minutes. Afterwards, without a word of explanation, he packed the chain saw back in his boot and drove away.

I confess also to succumbing to a sense of fear. My fear is that we might have become too much part of this buried landscape to ever adapt successfully back to city ways.

Perhaps, I speculate, my life skills have been less supplemented, more lost out here in the country, in the same way that a footballer loses his touch without consistent practice. Can a person be a virtual hermit then return to mainstream life with the same social confidence? Huge amounts of money would allow one to stand above the fundamental problems of both country and city life. Money may give rise to a whole plethora of other difficulties, I don't know, but it obviously relieves the grind, the drives, the pressures of life in the slowest lane. In our less than financially carefree position, how much of a problem will moving from the edge back to the centre be?

Will it be possible as a forty-something old fart to walk into a situation and say 'employ me, I may look long in the tooth (someone told me that I looked over-the-hill at twenty seven), I may have been living on a mountain for the past few years, but I still know how it all works ...'

I could go on and on, and as this is my epitaph to Ireland, perhaps I should. Living in the disadvantaged Irish countryside has been like living in a Dostoyevsky novel: the poverty, the religion, the alcohol, the bleak weather, the hard landscape, the history – all underwritten by desperation and tragedy. This is not solely my observation, I was first put up to it by a doctor in the town. He had set up an organisation to bring children from Chernobyl in Russia to Ireland each summer for a 'clean' holiday, away from the nuclear pollution causing untold mutative horror. We discussed at length the similarities between the two peoples, the Irish and the Russians. Now, I love all those novels by Turgenev, Gogol, Gorky and Chekhov. But I have to ask myself whether I want to live with Alyosha, Mr.Chichikov, Raskolnikov or Ivan and the answer is a very definite nyet, I'm very happy that they're safely tucked up in the pages of those books.

So it's farewell to Ireland. I know that when the car winds down this lonely track for the last time Clare and I will shed real tears and I am not looking forward to that ride. We have been irreversibly touched by this experience, and one can't exorcise it now. There are no regrets, quite the opposite. I know that whatever happens next, I will react to it with the benefit of an added perspective and perhaps a greater determination, a greater sense of responsibility, because I now know that rejecting the world is not an option.

Until next time....and from a different place.....

Tim.

ABOUT THE AUTHOR

Tim Haynes was born in South Africa during the dreaded Apartheid era. He attended a traditional boy's school, King Edward VII, and excelled at sport and not quite so much at studying. Never one to respect authority, his conflicts with the powers that were really blossomed during his compulsory service in the South African Army. He decided to quit his native land in 1975, returning with his family in 1995 after the New South Africa came into being.

Tim is a successful real estate developer in Johannesburg and now a reasonably responsible citizen. Yes, Clare is still at his side. Ciaran is in business with Tim. Gina lives in London.

His other books include "Stories of An Ordinary Misfit" and "KES AND TELL: The Untold Truth About King Edward VII School" (co-editor). You can reach Tim at timh@uptownprojects.co.za.

www.ingramcontent.com/pod-product-compliance
Lightning Source LLC
Chambersburg PA
CBHW051724040426

42447CB00008B/966